Brain Boost Formula

---

44 Brain Hacks
For Increasing Mental Clarity, Energy and Focus

By Chaz Wolfson

Over 60 scientific studies referenced

Chaz Wolfson

Disclaimers & Uses

Table of Contents

Part One

Chaz's Story

It was a sunny Tuesday afternoon back in 2015, a moment that remains vividly etched in my memory. I found myself lying on the patient bed in the doctor's office, and together, we examined the ultrasound results. With empathy in his eyes, the doctor gently uttered those life-altering words, "You have cancer."

That instant left an indelible mark on me, I was shocked and in disbelief that this could happen at this age. I was in the prime of my early 20s and realized there was now a battle at my front door. I could face the fear and move forward or pull away into despair. I'm proud of how I handled it.

In the years that followed, I grappled with exhaustion, brain fog, frequent headaches, and a lack of focus. My 20s were supposed to be some of the most vibrant and fulfilling years of my life. Instead, each day felt like a battle between my aspirations and the limitations imposed by my body.

However, my life took a turn for the better when I stumbled upon the world of biohacking and discovered ancient wisdom on how to create a healthy body. It was a revelation that allowed me to regain control over my energy, vitality, cognitive function, and productivity.

Since then, I have dedicated myself to refining the knowledge I gained and delving deep into the realms of health and wellness. My burning desire was to understand the root causes of my struggles, to never relive those painful moments, and to extend a helping hand to others, sparing them from similar hardships.

As a personal trainer, speaker, coach, and author in the health and fitness industry, I have had the privilege of positively impacting the lives of countless individuals. Guiding them towards healthier lifestyles and overall well-being has been immensely fulfilling.

Currently pursuing a Master's degree in physiology and kinesiology, equipped with numerous certifications in the health and fitness arena, and having written over 70 articles in the health space, I continue to embark on this weaving path.

This book is what I've learned about brain fog and low energy. It's not a dissertation of every cause of brain fog or a neurologist's handbook to neurotransmitters. I'm not a neuroscientist or a brain surgeon and I haven't conducted extensive studies on optimizing brain performance.

What this book offers is what I've found to be major culprits of brain fog and what to do about it, based on my own experiences and a decade of seeking answers. It showcases stories from my life and detailing my battles with brain fog. I also share some of the "brain biohacks" that I've found particularly effective. This is a testament to over 10 years of navigating and problem-solving outside the confines of traditional medical approaches, searching for my own clarity. Your journey might find a companion in mine.

I thank you for allowing me to share my story with you and for joining me on this incredible journey of growth and transformation. I believe that people like you and me will transform our society and culture as it is now into a better world. A world where we aren't plagued with so many chronic health conditions. And a world where our bodies are honored for the incredible cosmic masterpieces they are.

Getting Boosted

So, what exactly is the formula for enhancing brain function? For "Boosting a Brain?" I'm not sure there is one truth out there to universally help people boost their brain. But what I've found is that asking certain questions help. Questions such as, "Why?" Why does my energy seem to wane so quickly? What are the mechanisms that might be bringing me down? What can I do to get past this?

These questions have been my companions for almost a decade, guiding my journey of exploration. Everything I've shared in this book stems from my personal search for answers. It's a collection of insights I've gathered over the years, aiming to solve my own puzzles. Though I don't claim to have all the solutions and no single research paper encapsulates everything, I've meticulously selected and referenced over 60 top-notch sources.

So, what's the formula? Based on my findings, this is The Brain Boost Formula:

- Maximizing **Quality Input**
- Optimizing **Cellular Signaling**
- Beneficially adjusting our **Homeostasis**

In simpler terms, it suggests that we need to feed our bodies with the right nutrients and stimulate them with the correct cellular signals to shift our body's homeostasis, culminating in a heightened, "boosted" state.

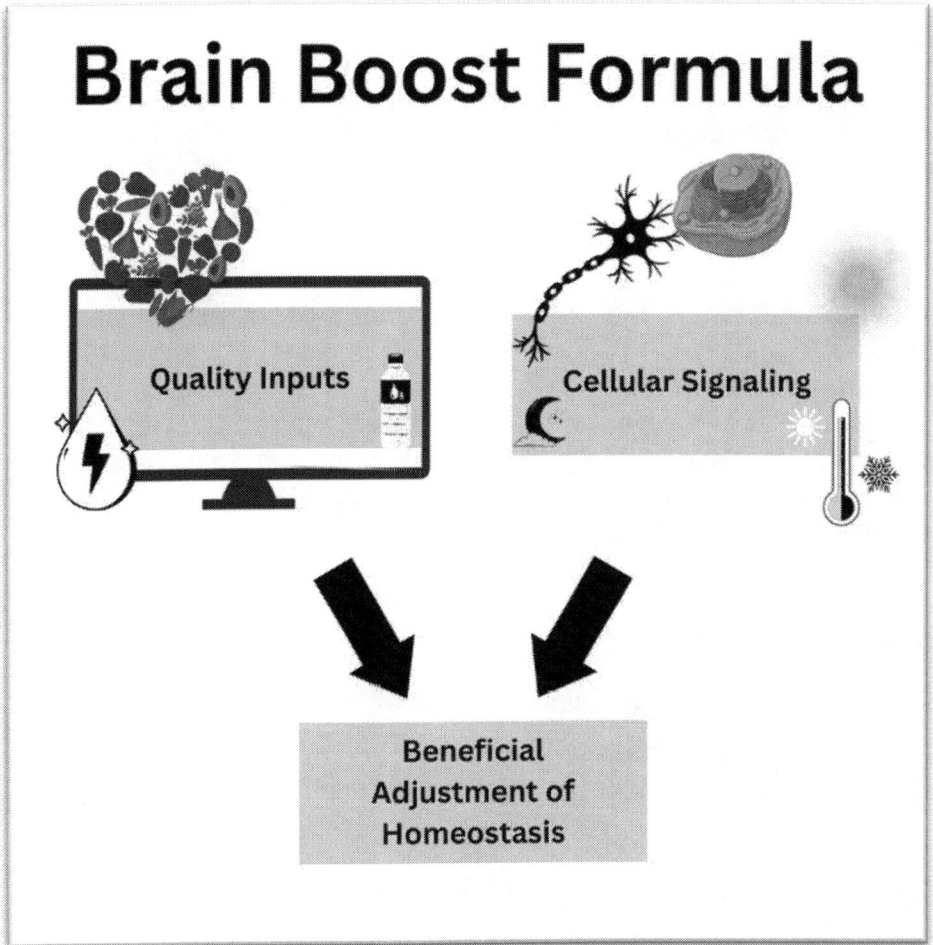

Brain Boost Formula

Quality Inputs

Cellular Signaling

Beneficial Adjustment of Homeostasis

For instance, consider this:

Input: The foods we consume, the water we drink, the balance of electrolytes, and the content we read, watch, or listen to.

Cellular signaling: Our body reacts to our environment, so if we can adjust the environment to signal what we want to our cells then we can ultimately create health in the body. 'Cellular signaling' is the stimuli we experience, such as temperature changes (cold or heat), light exposure, physical movement, auditory cues, and our sleep patterns.

The goal? To recalibrate our body's natural equilibrium, raising our overall energy levels to achieve a "boosted" state.

That leads to the next question, "What is a boosted state?"

A boosted state is a bit of a vague statement. We know when we're in it though. We have high energy levels, clear thinking and an almost instantaneous transition from thinking to acting.

For instance, I once worked at a recruitment firm where the norm was about 50 calls daily. On some days, the mere thought of calling "individual A" would be met with procrastination on my part. Maybe I'd engage in a casual chat with a colleague or handle some paperwork. Essentially, I'd dawdle before finally making the call.

Yet, on some days, it felt different. My cognition seemed keener, my energy surged, and upon deciding to make calls, I'd just do it. The process was direct: from the thought to the action. No hesitations, no lags, no sluggishness.

This elevated state is what we can induce by managing our bodily intake and communicating the right signals to our cellular structure. It's a mode where we're deeply anchored in the now, operating at our peak proficiency and self-assuredness.

Now can I promise this book will put you in a boosted state of supreme confidence and worthiness? Of course not. I'd be skeptical of anyone guaranteeing me such results.

Instead, this book is meant to help guide you towards finding that state for yourself. My hope for you is that you have a few key takeaways that help you focus a little bit more. That helps you find some way to increase your energy levels. And that you understand more about what could be causing brain fog in the first place so you can do something about it. Instead of possibly feeling helpless, as I felt years ago.

I hope that as you progress through this book, you'll find the tools, insights, and inspiration you need. More than anything, I want you to recognize that you are not alone in this journey. Many have walked this path before and have emerged with a clearer mind and a brighter spirit. With determination and a bit of guidance, you too can find your way to an elevated state, experiencing life with clarity, purpose, and vigor.

In the ensuing chapters, we'll explore the pressing significance of brain health in today's context. We'll then tackle the 7 Trolls of Brain Fog—the primary culprits behind brain fog that many of us inadvertently encounter. Following this, I'll share 44 brain "biohacks" that have not only stood the test of my personal experience but are also backed by scientific research. These hacks aim to amplify energy, sharpen mental clarity, and enhance focus, all integral to a flourishing state of mind.

As we journey through this book, I'll explain how this formula finds its manifestation in the real world, emphasizing its contemporary significance and application.

The Need for Prioritizing Brain Health in Today's Fast-Paced World

Today's world is fast-paced, demanding, and full of distractions. Now we have social media platforms bombarding us with notifications 24/7 on our mobile devices that are always with us. With screens in every room able to grab our attention away from the important things in life. And the best streaming shows this world has to offer! (Where's my Mandalorian and Last of Us fans??)

You know the story but it's worth repeating because we are all busy and it's easy to neglect our brain health. However, prioritizing brain health is more important now than ever before. Here's why.

First and foremost, the brain is the control center of the body. It's where your presence and awareness live. It's where our thoughts, emotions, and behaviors come to life. Taking care of our brain health is essential for a clear mind, effective decision-making, and overall well-being. It wasn't until my late 20s that I truly appreciated the impact our brain has on our daily experiences and how it shapes our world.

I was born in the 1990s, and by that time a shift in our culture had already been underway for decades. Poor brain health doesn't just come up, there's a reason we're seeing a decline in cognitive function at all ages. And it's not only tied to brain health alone.

Back in the 1960s, when everyone was grooving to The Beatles and we were dreaming of exploring outer space, the average weight of men in the United States was lighter compared to today. According to old records from the Metropolitan Life Insurance Company, men back then weighed around 166 to 170 pounds (75 to 77 kilograms).

But fast forward to today, and things have definitely changed. Over the past few decades, the average weight of American men has been steadily increasing. According to the Centers for Disease Control and Prevention (CDC), in 2018, the average weight of adult men aged 20 years and older was around 198.6 pounds (about 90 kilograms). That's quite a leap! About a 30-pound jump. Imagine 60 ribeye steaks weighing about 8 ounces each sitting on the kitchen table. That's how much we're talking about here.

This information comes from the CDC's National Health and Nutrition Examination Survey (NHANES), a program that looks into various health indicators, including weight.

The rise in obesity in America is a complex issue with many interconnected factors. It's a big web that involves different aspects of the food system, lifestyle choices, socioeconomic influences, corporate greed, and individual behaviors. Let's take a closer look at this societal gossamer.

Over the years, there has been an abundance of processed and calorie-dense foods. Fast food chains, convenience stores, and heavily marketed packaged goods have become extremely prevalent, making it easier for people to choose unhealthy options. And those processed foods often come with a lower price tag compared to fresh produce, which can impact our dietary decisions, especially for those with limited financial resources.

The food industry also plays a role in perpetuating these unhealthy habits. They use sophisticated marketing strategies to entice us with promises of greater value and satisfaction. However, this abundance may come at the expense of our waistlines and overall well-being.

Take a look at some cereals, for example. They may have a heart on the box, suggesting a healthy start to the day. But when you actually examine the nutrition label, you'll find minimal protein, high sugar, low fiber, and a lineup of processed ingredients. Growing up I ate those cereal boxes, thinking I was eating a healthy breakfast. Little did I know I being lied to by these companies that made this "food." Later in the book we'll touch on nutrition and what to do instead.

But as time went on, breakfast began to change. The Industrial Revolution brought shifts in work patterns and lifestyles, leading to a need for quick and convenient options. Enter the rise of ready-to-eat cereals, which gained popularity for their convenience and accessibility. Yet, these cereals often came packed with added sugars and flavors that appealed to our taste buds but did little for our health.

As the years passed, the breakfast landscape continued to evolve. The fast-food industry exploded, introducing breakfast sandwiches, pancakes, and sugary pastries that catered to our on-the-go lifestyles. It came with a side of extra calories and not-so-great ingredients. We started trading in nutrition for speed. Trans fats, sugars, and a bunch of stuff that's hard to pronounce started becoming breakfast regulars.

And it's not just breakfast that has changed. Portion sizes, too, have experienced a growth spurt of their own. When you go to a restaurant nowadays, it's not uncommon to find portions that could feed a small village. Back in the day, a regular soda was, what, 8 ounces? Now, the "medium" size at many places is closer to 20 ounces. Have you noticed how dinner plates seem to have stretched out over time too? They've become these vast, ceramic expanses that we feel compelled to fill. The old "eyes bigger than your stomach" saying has never felt more real.

And let's not forget about the grocery store aisles, where packages seem to have inflated alongside our expectations. Modest bags of chips have turned into family-sized packs, tempting us to consume more than necessary. I don't know about you but I can't stop eating after one serving of chips. It hits all my taste buds perfectly to keep me acting like Popeye for potato chips.

This "portion distortion" messes with our minds, making us believe that these super-sized portions are the new normal. Our internal portion compass seems to have gone haywire, causing us to lose touch with what a balanced serving should actually be. And the result? We end up consuming more calories, regardless of whether the food itself is healthy or not. Our bodies don't discriminate between a nutritious meal and an indulgent treat – they store those surplus calories, potentially leading to weight gain and related health issues.

Unhealthy fats have also contributed to the obesity epidemic. Trans fats, commonly found in fried and processed foods, have been shown to increase the risk of heart disease. That's why the World Health Organization (WHO) has taken a strong stance against them. In 2018, they launched the REPLACE initiative, aiming to eliminate artificial trans fats from the global food supply by 2023. Several countries have already implemented policies to restrict or ban trans fats, leading to a reduction in consumption and improved cardiovascular health.

But this isn't limited to the United States alone. It has become a global concern as countries around the world face similar patterns and challenges. That's why it's important to recognize that this is a shared fight, a worldwide struggle for our health, brain power, longevity, and overall quality of life.

As obesity levels continue to rise and the average weight of individuals increases, the prevalence of nutrient-poor diets and the consumption of processed foods become the norm. This pattern directly impacts brain health, as these diets are often deficient in essential nutrients necessary for optimal cognitive function. The combined effect of excessive caloric intake, inadequate nutrition, gut disruption and the negative impact of unhealthy fats creates a perfect storm for compromised brain health.

With compromised brain health, that ends up creating what's called brain fog. It's been a more popularized word that refers to the cognitive difficulties and lack of mental clarity experienced by individuals; we'll further break down exactly what brain fog is in the upcoming section. Brain fog can manifest as difficulty concentrating, memory problems, decreased productivity, and overall cognitive sluggishness. It can have a significant impact on daily functioning, affecting work performance, academic achievements, and personal relationships.

The link between obesity, poor dietary choices, and brain fog is becoming increasingly evident. The consumption of processed foods, high in sugars, unhealthy fats, and additives, can contribute to inflammation and oxidative stress in the brain. These physiological changes, combined with the potential nutrient deficiencies resulting from a poor diet, can impair neurotransmitter function and compromise the delicate balance of brain chemicals essential for optimal cognitive performance.

The brain relies on a steady supply of oxygen and nutrients delivered through healthy blood vessels, and any disruption in this process can negatively impact cognitive function.

Before going any further, it's crucial to understand the significance of brain health and gain a basic understanding of how the brain functions. By comprehending the inner workings of the brain and its role in our lives, we can gain a clearer perspective on its importance.

Brain health is essential for overall well-being and optimal functioning. A healthy brain enables us to think clearly, concentrate effectively, and learn new information. It supports emotional well-being, facilitates good decision-making, and helps us navigate our daily lives.

When the brain is not functioning optimally, it can lead to a range of cognitive, emotional, and behavioral challenges. Impaired brain health can manifest as difficulties with memory, attention, concentration, problem-solving, and mood regulation. It can impact our ability to perform tasks, affect our relationships, and diminish our quality of life.

The brain is divided into three main parts: the cerebrum, cerebellum, and brainstem. The cerebrum is the largest part of the brain, responsible for conscious thought, learning, and perception. The cerebellum is located below the cerebrum and is responsible for coordination and balance. The brainstem is located below the cerebellum and connects the brain to the spinal cord. It controls vital functions such as breathing, heart rate, and blood pressure.

The brain also has neurons, the building blocks of the brain, which communicate with each other through electrical and chemical signals; known as neurotransmitters. This intricate network of interconnected neurons forms pathways and circuits that allow for the transmission and processing of information.

There are many different types of neurotransmitters in the nervous system, each with a specific function. Some neurotransmitters, such as dopamine and serotonin, are involved in regulating mood, emotion, and behavior. Others, such as acetylcholine and norepinephrine, are involved in controlling movement, attention, and muscle activity. Still, others, such as GABA, act as a natural "brake" that inhibits or slows down the firing of neurons, helping to calm and relax the nervous system.

Disruptions in the balance of neurotransmitters in the brain can lead to neurological and psychiatric disorders, such as Parkinson's disease, depression, and schizophrenia. Disruptions can also lead to fatigue, low energy, or poor concentration. To understand neurotransmitters, we can use an analogy like communication between friends. The friends represent neurons or target cells that need to communicate.

The letters symbolize neurotransmitters, the chemical messages exchanged by neurons. Just as friends use letters to share information, neurons use neurotransmitters to transmit information.

The synaptic gap is like a postal service, bridging the space between neurons. It's where neurotransmitters are released and travel to reach their destination, just as the postal service carries letters between friends.

Addresses and stamps on letters are akin to receptors on the receiving neuron or target cell. Like correct addresses and stamps ensure delivery, neurotransmitters must bind to specific receptors for effective communication.

Reading the letter corresponds to the changes that occur in the receiving cell once neurotransmitters bind to receptors. This enables the receiving neuron or target cell to process and respond to the information conveyed by neurotransmitters.

Overall, neurons and neurotransmitters are essential components of the nervous system, allowing for the transmission of information throughout the body. Neurons transmit electrical signals and release neurotransmitters, which bind to receptors on other neurons or target cells to trigger further signaling.

Now, to answer the most important question of clear cognitive function, "What causes brain fog?" Let's dive in.

The Seven Trolls of Brain Fog

For most of my life, I've felt like my brain hasn't been as clear as everyone else's. It's felt lethargic and sluggish compared to family members, friends and peers. That pushed me to ask why. Why was my brain not up to par? Why wasn't I as energetic as I know I could be? Those questions lead me down many rabbit holes.

I first started with the psychological side of the brain. I dug into the research and read many books about how our thoughts can impact our energy levels. When I was a teenager I didn't know I could think differently. I thought my thoughts were a part of me, they were me! It wasn't until I read the book "The Power of Now" by Eckart Tolle did I realize I had the power to be the observer of my thoughts.

That changed the game for me. It put me in the driver's seat of my own mind whereas before that I felt at the mercy of whatever behaviors came. More on this later.

So the psychology side of the brain was the first I dug deep into. After several years of reading dozens more books on that subject, I started looking into the physical side of the body. I thought, "Well I've done a lot of work on the psychological end but still have a lack of brain power, maybe it's more biologically related."

That pointed me in the direction to continue to learn more about the causes of brain fog. I came to these main seven areas of the body and mind in what I call 'The Seven Trolls of Brain Fog'. I've identified these seven areas as the biggest influences on brain fog. So, what is brain fog?

"Brain fog" is a catch-all term that captures a range of cognitive difficulties, including:

- Memory Issues: This could be short-term memory lapses, forgetfulness, or difficulty recalling names or facts.
- Lack of Focus: Difficulty concentrating on tasks, being easily distracted, or finding it hard to maintain attention on one thing.
- Reduced Mental Clarity: Feeling as if thoughts are "hazy" or "clouded," leading to challenges in decision-making or problem-solving.
- Fatigue: A pervasive sense of mental fatigue, even after a full night's sleep.
- Slow Thinking: A sensation of slowed down thought processes, taking longer to process information or respond.

I chose to boil it down to these seven causes as they're also some of the biggest ones we have control over. By no means is this an exhaustive list and these seven also exclude any serious medical conditions that might be going on; such as diabetes or lime disease. This is also not a medical article on the exact causes of brain fog and every possible reason. It's very much what I've experienced and learned over the years. I'm simply sharing what I've come across. And of course, if you have any medical questions please consult with your physician.

Let's dive into one of the biggest ones I've struggled with in my life and what's becoming the popular kid on the block; gut health.

Tummy Troll: The Gut-Brain Axis

Without discussing the gut-brain axis, this book would be incomplete. The reason is that my journey towards better health began with trying to resolve my gut issues. Over the years, I have struggled with various gut problems such as IBS, Inflammatory Bowel Disease, slow gut motility, gluten sensitivity, and leaky gut. I didn't have these issues as a kid though, they came on because of a few reasons. First and foremost is from the power of the mind.

Growing up, I never really experienced anxiety. There were times when I felt introverted or shy during my youth, but it wasn't a chronic issue for me. However, when I graduated from UF in 2013 and moved to San Francisco at the age of 23, things took a different turn, and I began to experience physical manifestations of chronic anxiety.

The transition to a new job, a new life, and a new place with new roommates brought about significant changes. The sheer magnitude of these changes overwhelmed me and caused excessive stress, which, in turn, took a toll on my gut. Additionally, I wasn't taking proper care of my body. I indulged in heavy beer and alcohol consumption from Thursday to Sunday, often consuming six or more drinks each night. Late-night fast food binges followed these drinking sessions, and I even smoked cigars and other tobacco products during that time. Consequently, I woke up with hangovers and headaches the next day, reminiscent of Stu's experiences in "The Hangover."

The pain reliever pills I relied on to alleviate the hangover symptoms sometimes irritated and disrupted my gut function. The combination of physical and mental stress created a perfect storm, resulting in my gut going haywire. As my gut health deteriorated, I began to notice an increase in anxiety, which became more prominent with each passing day.

After a few months of enduring digestive issues, I decided to consult a gastroenterologist. The doctor conducted tests to check for a wheat allergy, and to my surprise, the results came back positive. The gastroenterologist advised me to avoid wheat in my diet. Unfortunately, what happened afterward is a bit hazy in my memory. Either the doctor didn't provide me with a proper plan, or perhaps I failed to follow up on the consultation. Regardless, I didn't receive much help or relief for my persistent gut pain, except for the advice to abstain from the foods I was addicted to, including the wheat-based products, and to cut back on my reliance on beer.

At that time, I was aware that wheat sometimes caused discomfort in my gut, but I was young, reckless and felt invincible. I shrugged off the occasional upset stomach, thinking I was tougher than that. I was determined not to let a mere bellyache hinder me from having my share of fun. For about 18 months, I continued to indulge in excessive drinking, smoking, and overconsumption of wheat products.

Then, everything changed with a sudden and devastating diagnosis: cancer. The big "C." At just 24 years old, I felt like I had been transported to another dimension like I was trapped in the Twilight Zone. The reality of the situation seemed surreal, and I couldn't help but think, "This can't be really happening."

I ended up going through chemo in 2015, at the age of 24. And was pronounced free and clear by 25. But my gut problems still lingered in my core.

These issues led me to delve deeper into the connection between the gut and the brain and how they influence each other. Therefore, understanding the gut-brain axis has been instrumental in my personal health journey, and is crucial when on the mission to get clearer thinking and better concentration.

The idea that the gut and the brain are connected may sound surprising at first, but recent research has revealed a complex and bidirectional communication network between the two organs. This relationship, known as the gut-brain axis, has important implications for our overall health and well-being. I'm not a gut researcher but here are some of the things I've learned about it.

The gut-brain axis refers to the bidirectional communication system between the gut and the brain. This communication occurs through various pathways, including neural, hormonal, and immune signals. The gut and the brain are connected by the vagus nerve, which is the longest nerve in the body and serves as a direct conduit for information between the two organs.

The vagus nerve, also known as the tenth cranial nerve is a crucial part of the autonomic nervous system. It's the longest and most complex cranial nerve, extending from the brainstem to various organs throughout the body. While the vagus nerve is not directly part of the enteric nervous system (ENS), there is an important connection between the two.

The enteric nervous system is a complex network of nerves located within the walls of the gastrointestinal tract. It functions independently of the central nervous system (CNS) but can communicate with it. The ENS is responsible for regulating and coordinating many aspects of digestive function, including motility (movement of food through the digestive system), secretion of digestive enzymes and hormones, and blood flow to the gastrointestinal organs.

Although the vagus nerve does not physically pass through the enteric nervous system, it plays a vital role in modulating its activity. The vagus nerve has both afferent (sensory) and efferent (motor) fibers. The afferent fibers of the vagus nerve transmit sensory information from the gastrointestinal tract to the brain, allowing the brain to monitor the status of digestion and make appropriate adjustments.

Conversely, the fibers of the vagus nerve carry signals from the brain to the enteric nervous system, influencing its function. This bidirectional communication enables the vagus nerve to regulate various aspects of gastrointestinal activity, including motility, secretion, and inflammation.

For example, when the brain detects that food has entered the stomach, it can send signals via the vagus nerve to stimulate gastric acid secretion and promote the rhythmic contractions of the stomach muscles, which aid in digestion. Conversely, during times of stress or during the "rest and digest" phase of the autonomic nervous system, the vagus nerve can send inhibitory signals to slow down gastric activity and promote relaxation of the gastrointestinal muscles.

It is believed that the vagus nerve transmits signals from the gut to the brain, influencing various aspects of brain function, including mood, behavior, and even cognition. This connection has implications for understanding the link between gastrointestinal disorders and mental health conditions.

In my opinion, this is also a big part of where the "stomach butterfly" vernacular originated from. If you aren't aware, having a "butterfly" effect in the stomach region is stated when one is about to do something they're feeling nervous about. For example, if someone is about to perform a public speaking presentation they may get "butterflies" in their stomach before going up to speak. I believe this is due to the gut-brain connection that's going on. So, as the brain is feeling nervous and stressed, those signals are passed down to the gut. And within gut health contains, figurative, microscopic butterflies I've come to learn much more about over the years.

The gut contains trillions of bacteria, collectively known as the gut microbiota, which play a crucial role in maintaining gut health and regulating the gut-brain axis. These bacteria produce various chemicals, including neurotransmitters, that can influence brain function and behavior. For example, serotonin, a neurotransmitter that regulates mood, is produced both in the gut and the brain, and disruptions in the gut microbiota can lead to altered serotonin levels and symptoms of depression and anxiety.

Moreover, the gut microbiota can modulate the immune system and regulate inflammation, which is implicated in many neurological disorders, including Alzheimer's disease, Parkinson's disease, and multiple sclerosis. The gut microbiota can also affect the production of short-chain fatty acids, which are important for gut health, and can cross the blood-brain barrier and affect brain function.

Imbalances in gut bacteria have been linked to a range of mental health issues, from mood disorders like depression and anxiety to neurodevelopmental disorders like autism. In the review 'Gut microbiota's effect on mental health: The gut-brain axis' by Clapp M and team, they state the following:

"This review demonstrates the importance of a healthy microbiome, particularly the gut microbiota, for patients suffering from anxiety and depression, as dysbiosis and inflammation in the CNS have been linked as potential causes of mental illness."

When my gut is acting up and I'm feeling extra bloated I can feel it influence my mood. In my 20's, when my gut was at its worst, I had unexplainable anxiety; or so I thought at the time. I came to find out later that because my gut was in such dysbiosis it probably impacted my mood often. I'm sure there were other things happening but it didn't feel like a purely psychological issue. It felt physical. Like my body was physically manifesting anxiety. It was the oddest feeling and a horrible one at that because I couldn't find a way to solve it until I started looking deeper into gut health.

The gut-brain axis also plays a role in regulating appetite and metabolism. The gut produces hormones, such as ghrelin and leptin, that signal to the brain when to eat and when to stop eating. Disruptions in this signaling can lead to overeating and obesity.

Recent studies have also suggested that the gut-brain axis may be involved in the development of certain psychiatric and neurological disorders, including autism, schizophrenia, and depression. Researchers are investigating the potential for gut microbiota-targeted therapies, such as probiotics, prebiotics, and fecal microbiota transplantation, as a way to modulate the gut-brain axis and improve outcomes for these disorders.

LPS

Disruptions in the gut-brain axis can lead to various issues. One such problem is when lipopolysaccharides (LPS), which are components of the outer membrane of certain bacteria, enter the bloodstream through a phenomenon known as "leaky gut." In a healthy gut, the intestinal barrier acts as a defense mechanism, preventing the entry of harmful substances like LPS into the bloodstream.

When the intestinal barrier becomes compromised, as is the case with a leaky gut, LPS can pass through and enter the bloodstream. Once in the bloodstream, LPS can potentially reach the nervous system, including the brain. This can trigger an immune response and cause inflammation in the brain, leading to a range of neurological and mental health issues.

The presence of LPS in the nervous system can activate immune cells, such as microglia, leading to neuroinflammation. Neuroinflammation has been linked to various conditions, including anxiety, depression, cognitive impairment, and neurodegenerative disorders.

To maintain a healthy gut-brain axis and prevent the entry of LPS into the nervous system, it's crucial to support gut health and promote a strong intestinal barrier.

Overall, the gut-brain axis is a complex and dynamic communication system that regulates various physiological processes, including mood, appetite, and metabolism. The gut microbiota plays a crucial role in this relationship, and disruptions in gut health can lead to altered brain function and behavior. Therefore, watering down our excitement for life at times. Speaking of water…

Water Troll: The Primordial Element Imbalance

Ancient civilizations recognized the importance of water for survival, but the understanding of its composition and properties evolved over time.

In ancient Greece, the philosopher Thales of Miletus held a profound belief that water served as the fundamental substance from which all things in the universe originated. Thales, known as one of the Seven Sages of Greece, lived during the 6th century BCE and made significant contributions to various fields, including philosophy, mathematics, and astronomy. He was so impactful that Aristotle later referred to his work.

Thales' perspective on water as the primordial element stemmed from his observation of the world around him. He noticed the essential role that water played in sustaining life, its omnipresence in nature, and its transformative properties. This led him to propose that water was the fundamental building block from which everything else emerged.

Thales' concept of water as the fundamental substance had both philosophical and scientific implications. Philosophically, his viewpoint suggested unity and interconnectedness among all things. Water, in its various forms, could transform into solid ice, evaporate into gaseous vapor, and flow as liquid, symbolizing the dynamic nature of existence.

Scientifically, Thales' notion laid the foundation for future philosophers and natural philosophers to explore the nature of reality and investigate the fundamental elements that compose the universe. His elemental theory opened the door to further inquiries into the nature of matter and the search for underlying principles that governed the cosmos.

Even today, we look back at philosophers like Thales and think we've come a long way. However, 2,000 years from now civilization will look back on us having discovered the internet for example; and meanwhile, they'll be creating their hologram books on planet Proxima Centauri b in another solar system.

So what does this have to do with brain fog? The importance of water for our world and bodies cannot be understated. However, today people are still under drinking water and, what we'll talk about later in this section, electrolytes.

Water is vital to our brain's ability to function properly. A dehydrated brain isn't working at 100% capacity.

In the study, "Effects of mild dehydration on cognitive function in healthy young women" published in the Journal of Nutrition by Armstrong, et al., the team wanted to see how hydration affected the brain.

To conduct the study, they recruited 12 healthy women, aged around 26 years, with an average BMI of 22.5. They divided the study into different sessions. The first one was a control session (CON) where the participants kept track of what they ate and drank and their physical activity using a diary and a Fitbit®. Then, they had two other sessions: one where the women deliberately drank less water (dehydration or DEH session) and another where they drank the recommended daily amount of water for their age and sex (euhydration or EUH session), which was around 2500ml or 2.5 liters in 24 hours.

To measure cognitive function, the researchers used computer-based tests that checked emotion, sensory perception, and other cognitive abilities. They conducted these tests at different times during the day: 5 PM the night before the sessions (baseline or BL), and then at 7 AM, 12 PM, and 5 PM during the sessions.

The researchers found that urine-specific gravity (a measure of hydration) was similar at the baseline for all conditions. However as the dehydration session progressed, urine specific gravity increased, indicating that the participants were becoming more dehydrated.

When the participants drank enough water during the euhydration session, they actually improved their visual and working memory. There was also a positive impact on executive function (set shifting), showing fewer errors as the day went on under the euhydration condition.

Based on their findings, the researchers concluded that even mild dehydration could cause deficits in visual and working memory, as well as executive function, in healthy young women. However, these deficits were reversed when the women drank enough water, following the recommended daily intake of 2.5 liters/day for adult women as recommended by the European Food Safety Authority and Institute of Medicine.

In a nutshell, this study highlights the importance of staying hydrated, as it can significantly affect our cognitive abilities, like memory and decision-making skills.

Not only is it important to drink enough water but it's vital to ensure we're getting the electrolytes we need. In the 19th century, the concept of electrolytes emerged. Swedish chemist Svante Arrhenius proposed the theory of electrolytic dissociation, which explained that certain substances in water could dissociate into electrically charged particles called ions. This theory laid the foundation for our understanding of electrolytes as substances that conduct electricity when dissolved in water.

Further advancements in the understanding of electrolytes and their role in bodily functions came with the rise of modern physiology. In the early 20th century, scientists like Albert Szent-Györgyi and J.B. Sumner made important discoveries related to electrolytes and their impact on muscle contraction and nerve signaling.

Today, our understanding of water and electrolytes continues to evolve through ongoing research and medical advancements. Electrolyte imbalances are closely monitored in medical settings, and solutions containing electrolytes are commonly used for rehydration purposes, especially in cases of dehydration or fluid imbalance

A dry and malnourished brain can't create the spark it needs to have powerful thoughts. One of the main reasons people experience brain fog is simply being dehydrated. Drinking enough water is essential for optimal brain health.

Beyond just drinking enough water it ensures the right level of electrolytes in the body. If we're drinking enough water sometimes we're not taking in enough electrolytes with it. And if we drink too much water in a day we can actually wash out electrolytes from our system. To an extreme, and deadly, level we can experience hyponatremia.

Hyponatremia is a medical condition characterized by an abnormally low level of sodium in the blood. Sodium Is an essential electrolyte that helps regulate the balance of fluids in and around cells. When the concentration of sodium in the blood drops too low, it can disrupt the body's normal functions and lead to various symptoms, ranging from mild to severe.

One common cause of hyponatremia is excessive water intake without adequately replacing lost sodium. This can occur during prolonged and intense physical activities, like marathons or endurance events, where individuals drink large amounts of water to stay hydrated. When they sweat heavily, they lose both water and sodium from their bodies. If they consume too much water without replenishing the lost sodium, it can dilute the sodium levels in the blood, leading to hyponatremia.

I don't want to scare you as this most likely won't happen in our everyday lives. It's a condition that comes with long endurance events in hot weather where the participant drinks too much water without electrolytes in it. I do want to highlight this because of the importance of taking in electrolytes along with water.

Have you ever had several glasses of water but don't feel satisfied? Like you still need more water?

I feel this most of my life. For some reason, my brother, mother and I have a strong need to drink a lot of water. I believe it's a genetic condition because we all have it. Whenever I'm slamming back water after water I sometimes still don't feel hydrated. When that happens I have to take a second and think about my electrolyte consumption over the past 24 hours.

Sometimes my body isn't telling me to drink more water, it's telling me that I need more electrolytes. But the body can't decipher signals of thirst. It just gives a green light saying "Consume more!" I have to interpret that signal as "water" or "electrolytes" and act accordingly.

Before we go any further let's briefly go over electrolytes and what they do for us. Electrolytes are electrically charged minerals that play crucial roles in maintaining the balance of fluids both inside and outside our cells. They are essential for various physiological processes, including nerve function, muscle contractions, and maintaining the body's acid-base balance. The main electrolytes in our bodies are sodium, potassium, calcium, magnesium, chloride, bicarbonate, and phosphate.

Here's a brief overview of what these electrolytes do for us:

1. Sodium (Na+): Sodium is the most abundant positively charged ion outside the cells. It helps regulate the body's water balance, nerve impulses, and muscle contractions. It's also critical for maintaining blood pressure.
2. Potassium (K+): Potassium is the primary positively charged ion inside the cells. It plays a key role in muscle function, nerve transmission, and maintaining the electrical activity of the heart.

3. Calcium (Ca2+): Calcium is vital for building and maintaining strong bones and teeth. It also facilitates muscle contractions, blood clotting, and nerve function.
4. Magnesium (Mg2+): Magnesium is involved in more than 300 enzymatic reactions in the body. It helps with muscle and nerve function, maintaining a steady heartbeat, and supporting a healthy immune system.
5. Chloride (Cl-): Chloride is the most common negatively charged ion outside the cells. It works closely with sodium to help maintain proper fluid balance and osmotic pressure.
6. Bicarbonate (HCO3-): Bicarbonate plays a significant role in maintaining the body's acid-base balance (pH levels) and is involved in regulating carbon dioxide levels in the blood.
7. Phosphate (HPO42-): Phosphate is crucial for bone health, energy metabolism, and supporting various cellular functions.

In summary, they help keep our nerves firing correctly, our muscles moving as they should, and maintain the right balance of fluids in and around our cells.

We're getting better in the US, specifically, to drink more water in general. Too many people underdrink water and it leaves them dehydrated. But alongside the goal of drinking enough water to be what's called euhydrated (sufficiently hydrated), we also need to be including these electrolytes in our water. This can be done once a day it doesn't have to be in every glass. I'll go more into this in the brain hacks section in the later portion of this book. But the main takeaway from this chapter is that dehydration can be a cause of brain fog alongside not having enough electrolytes in our system.

In addition to the electrolytes circulating within our cells, it's crucial to monitor our hormone levels. Mine were way out of whack for too long. And with that said, let's look next at how our hormones can effect brain fog.

Endo Troll: Hormonal Imbalances

You've probably heard of the guy who has 22-inch arms, bacne, and a wicked temper who goes from engulfing protein pancakes to flipping the table over in an instant because the waiter said something that slightly upset the muscle man. What I'm talking about here is how hormones have an impact on our brain, mood and energy levels. This troll is named "Endo" because of its reference to the endocrine system.

The endocrine system is one of the most influential mechanisms on the brain's ability to function properly. Too often we throw pills, supplements, or other secondary, symptomatic treating, things at the problem of brain fog or fatigue when instead we need to be looking at someone's hormonal levels.

The early roots of endocrinology trace back to ancient China, even if they didn't have the specific scientific concepts or terminologies, like the "endocrine system", that we use today.

According to Traditional Chinese Medicine (TCM), the body is seen as a balance of two opposing yet interconnected forces, Yin and Yang. Yin represents elements that are calm, cold, and internal, while Yang represents elements that are active, hot, and external. Imbalances between these forces were seen as the cause of diseases. This Yin-Yang theory and the theory of the Five Elements were central to TCM's understanding of the body's functions and were applied to all aspects of health, including what we now understand as endocrinological functions.

The five elements, according to this theory, are Wood, Fire, Earth, Metal, and Water. These elements are believed to be the fundamental elements of the natural world and are associated with a wide range of phenomena and concepts. Each element is associated with certain energetic properties and they interact with each other in generative and controlling cycles.

As early as 200 BC, Chinese physicians were engaging in the isolation and use of hormones for medicinal purposes. Their pursuit of knowledge led them to explore the potential therapeutic benefits hidden within human urine. Through a series of intricate processes, they extracted hormones related to sex and the pituitary gland, opening the doors to the world of endocrinology.

The advancement of endocrinology did not solely belong to ancient China. In ancient Greece and Rome, skilled anatomists were making significant strides in identifying many relevant tissues and organs, including the endocrine glands. However, the prevailing theories during this period were more humoral in nature.

The humoral theory, famously proposed by the ancient Greek physician Hippocrates, suggested that the human body contained four essential fluids or "humors" - blood, phlegm, yellow bile, and black bile. Health and disease were thought to be a result of maintaining a balance of these humors. Although anatomists like Aristotle, Lucretius, Celsus, and Galen identified the endocrine glands, their understanding of their function and role in health and disease was limited.

In the 19th century, important discoveries laid the groundwork for endocrinology. Arnold Berthold's experiments with castrated cockerels (roosters) hinted at the role of testes in secreting substances that influenced male characteristics.

One day, as he gazed at a group of crowing cockerels in his yard, a question formed in his mind: 'what makes these birds exhibit their distinctly male behaviors?'

In 1849, Berthold then performed a groundbreaking experiment. He took two healthy cockerels and castrated them. After the castration, he observed that these birds lost several of their male behaviors. They no longer crowed, were less aggressive, and their combs and wattles (distinctive red flesh on their heads) shrunk. The castrated cockerels also didn't develop the typical male plumage.

However, Berthold's genius lay not only in observation but also in further experimentation. He took things a step further. He transplanted the testes from other roosters into the abdomen of the castrated cockerels. Astoundingly, the behaviors and physical characteristics that had vanished began to return.

From these experiments, Berthold made a pivotal conclusion: the testes must produce a substance that was vital for the male characteristics of the cockerel. He deduced that this substance, which we now know as testosterone, was being absorbed directly into the blood, influencing the body. This idea was revolutionary at the time. It laid the foundation for the concept of hormones – chemicals produced by glands in one part of the body that could travel through the bloodstream to exert effects on distant organs and tissues.

As word of Berthold's work spread, it spurred interest among other scientists, one by the name of Ernest Starling. They began to investigate other glands like the thyroid, adrenal glands, and the pancreas. This led to the identification of more hormones and a deeper understanding of their roles.

This eventually led to the coining of the term "hormone" by Ernest Starling, a British physiologist, in 1905. This term marked a crucial milestone in the study of the endocrine system, as it provided a unifying concept to describe a group of substances that played pivotal roles in communication and regulation within the body.

In 1921, the Austrian physiologist Otto Loewi conducted an experiment that marked a significant milestone in our understanding of neurotransmission and the communication between nerves and target tissues.

Loewi conducted an experiment using two live frog hearts, each contained within its own perfusion chamber. One of these hearts had its vagus nerve intact, while the other was denervated, meaning its nerve connection was severed. Loewi's experiment aimed to explore the effects of nerve signaling on heart function.

In the first part of the experiment, Loewi stimulated the vagus nerve connected to the first heart, resulting in a slower heart rate—a phenomenon already understood at that time. Interestingly, when Loewi transferred the perfusate (the liquid from the first heart's chamber) to the second heart, the second heart's rate also slowed down, mimicking the effect of vagus nerve stimulation. This indicated that a substance in the perfusate was responsible for transmitting the signal that influenced heart rate.

In a related experiment, Loewi demonstrated that transferring perfusate from a heart whose accelerator nerve was stimulated caused a second heart to beat more rapidly. This further supported the idea that the perfusate contained substances that could modulate heart rate.

Today, we know this substance as acetylcholine, a neurotransmitter that plays a crucial role in transmitting signals between nerves and target tissues.

By demonstrating that chemical substances released by nerves could influence the function of distant organs, he not only introduced the concept of neurotransmission but also opened the door to understanding the complex interplay between the nervous system, hormones, and bodily functions.

For his groundbreaking work, Loewi was awarded the Nobel Prize in Medicine. His experiment not only reshaped our understanding of how nerve cells communicate but also paved the way for further discoveries in neuroscience and the broader field of physiology.

The insights from Otto Loewi's experiment set the stage for further advancements in our understanding of how the nervous system communicates and collaborates with other systems in the body.

Two prominent figures whose pioneering work would usher in a new era of comprehension and exploration: Harvard-educated American physiologist Walter Cannon and the British neurosurgeon Geoffrey Harris.

Walter Cannon was born on October 19, 1871, in Prairie du Chien, Wisconsin, USA. He studied at Harvard University, where he received his bachelor's degree in 1896 and his medical degree in 1900. After completing his medical education, he pursued further studies in Europe, including work with eminent physiologists like Claude Bernard and Henry Dale.

Walter Cannon's contributions during the 1900s revolutionized our understanding of the brain's influence on hormonal control and introduced the concept of homeostasis.

He formulated the concept of homeostasis by building upon Claude Bernard's earlier idea of "milieu intérieur" and propagated it widely through his book "The Wisdom of the Body."

If you recall, The Brain Boost Formula has a "change in homeostasis." So this is explaining what homeostasis means broken down since Cannon has such an elaborate definition. This is a simplified version of what he wrote.

Cannon's Homeostasis:

1) Maintaining Constancy in Open Systems: Cannon believed that our bodies, like open systems, need special methods to stay balanced. He noticed how things like our sugar levels and body temperature are kept steady by our body's complex processes.

2) Counteracting Tendencies for Change: Cannon said our bodies have ways to resist changes. For example, when our blood sugar rises, we get thirsty to help dilute the sugar and bring balance.

3) Coordinated Mechanisms: Cannon explained that to keep everything in check, different parts of our body work together. Like with blood sugar, various hormones team up to control it.

4) Organized Self-Governance: Cannon underlined that homeostasis is not a random occurrence but a result of orderly self-regulation. It's because of well-organized processes that actively maintain stability.

Walter Cannon's conceptualization of homeostasis, further elaborated in "The Wisdom of the Body," demonstrated his capacity to distill complex physiological phenomena into clear and accessible terms. He connected Claude Bernard's foundational idea with practical observations and introduced a comprehensive framework for understanding how the body maintains stability with internal and external changes. This framework continues to underpin our understanding of physiological regulation and remains a cornerstone of modern biology.

Cannon's observations were not limited to isolated aspects of physiology but rather aimed at understanding the body's ability to maintain a state of internal balance despite external fluctuations. He recognized that the brain played a central role in orchestrating this equilibrium and ensuring that vital physiological processes remained within a narrow range conducive to optimal function.

Cannon's renowned research on the "fight or flight" response, carried out in collaboration with his colleagues, illuminated the intricate interplay between the brain, the sympathetic nervous system, and hormonal responses. He unveiled the body's remarkable ability to swiftly adapt to stressors by releasing hormones like adrenaline, which prepared the body for quick and decisive action. This discovery was a significant step forward in comprehending the brain's role in initiating hormonal responses and demonstrated how the nervous system and endocrine system collaborated to ensure survival and well-being.

While serving as a military doctor during World War I, Walter Cannon made a significant discovery – he noticed that the blood of soldiers in shock had become acidic. It's intriguing that we understood this concept almost a century ago.

Although not all of us are currently engaged in warfare, we can experience a similar physiological response to stress as soldiers do. Stress at work or in other areas of life can lead to the release of stress-related chemicals in our bodies, making our blood more acidic, much like what was observed in soldiers in the early 1900s. This is a vital element that we'll be discussing further in the upcoming troll chapter on our mental and psychological state of mind.

When I began my first corporate job after college at 23 years old in San Francisco, I took on a sales role. I encountered office politics, demanding deadlines, and long hours like never before, which was overwhelming. I struggled during the initial months.

The mistakes I made caused physical discomfort in my gut. The pressure of deadlines was intense. At that time, I lacked the skills, work endurance, and capabilities to handle such a high-pressure environment. The job demanded a lot with insufficient time and resources. Continuous stress became my affliction. Requests from colleagues, supervisors, and clients were ceaseless, eroding my personal boundaries. The stress negatively affected my sleep, further weakening my ability to manage stress and think clearly.

I'm sharing my experience because I believe I was facing a similar sensation of "shock" that soldiers undergo. I can't imagine dealing with what soldiers have to deal with. So by no means do I think I had a similar experience. Only that my body perceived my environment as a threat and reacted accordingly. Even in hindsight, I haven't encountered chronic stress like that since, as I do my utmost to avoid such situations.

I suspect that for about a year and a half, my body experienced heightened acidity due to imbalanced cortisol levels, catecholamines, and other hormones. This might make sense because, toward the end of those 18 months, I received a cancer diagnosis. Cancer thrives in an acidic and sugary environment. Stress doesn't guarantee cancer, but it might elevate the risk.

Cancer remains somewhat enigmatic to us. Our progress in technology and healthcare has been remarkable since medieval times and the early 1900s. However, we still have much to uncover about how our bodies function. In 500 years, our current understanding might be seen as primitive. There might even be people in the 2500s LARPing or imitating some aspects of our lives today as part of their games. But I'm getting off track. The point is, that we're still learning, and it's crucial to remain open-minded about our body's capabilities and how hormones can affect almost every system of our body. Speaking of which, let's jump back to the mid-1900s when Geoffrey Harris was making his discoveries and conclusions about the brain.

Across the Atlantic, Geoffrey Wingfield Harris (1913–1971) stood as a British physiologist and a paragon in the realm of neuroendocrinology. He was making pivotal contributions that further researched the critical relationship between the brain and the pituitary gland. Harris conducted experiments that involved manipulating the hypothalamus, a region of the brain situated just above the pituitary gland. Through his studies, Harris demonstrated that lesions in the hypothalamus could disrupt the delicate balance of hormonal regulation. This groundbreaking work underscored the brain's role as a master conductor, controlling the release of hormones from the pituitary gland and, by extension, influencing various bodily functions.

In this connected system, there's a repeating pattern: hormones go to the brain, making the brain tell the body to release specific hormones back. These hormones traveling in the body influence the brain too. This back-and-forth shows that while the brain controls the system, hormones could significantly impact the brain's ability to achieve mental clarity, maintain energy levels, and sustain focus. Let's now dive into what those hormones are and how they impact the brain.

Brain Hormones

At 25 years old, when the body was supposed to be at its peak state, my body felt at its most sluggish and poorest performing state. I experienced daily brain fog and slow thinking. I knew the brain wasn't supposed to feel this way and that my body felt lethargic. Trying to get through a full day of work was brutal. It was me against my body every hour.

It wasn't until a few years later did I start to get more into understanding the body and why I may have felt that way. I searched everywhere I could to find an answer to why and how to fix this. All that curiosity and desperation led me to hormones' impact on the brain. It first began when I saw a hormone doctor and we tested my thyroid and testosterone levels. Both are very low, diagnosed with hypothyroidism, not surprising.

We worked on getting my thyroid better and after taking medications to help my thyroid I was shocked at how much better I felt each day. Where I'd normally have an afternoon dip in energy now I'm able to have 10 or more productive hours in a day. It's not all due to the thyroid but after I got my levels checked and did something about it things really changed.

Now, not everyone will have such a clear answer as "Take this thyroid medication and your energy will go up." This is because sometimes people's thyroids are fine and they still feel brain fog. That's why there are six more trolls and not just this one. But, hormones are more broad than just thyroid hormones. And if you've never had your hormone levels checked or it's been several years I recommend you see an endocrinologist in your area to work on that. It can be eye-opening to finally be able to get a clear answer.

There's a lot that goes on in the brain and I'm not going to cover every hormone or neurotransmitter and mechanism of action in this chapter. That would be too boring for you, and me, and unnecessary. Instead, I'm going to focus on a few hormones that play a big role in regulating brain function.

Now, it's important to note that I'm only going to discuss a couple of hormones, not ones that can act as neurotransmitters too. For example, dopamine is a hormone and neurotransmitter. I'll briefly discuss it but the main three hormones that I've found to have the biggest impact on the brain are testosterone, thyroid hormones and cortisol. By no means is this an exhaustive list and by changing one hormone you will certainly have a cascade of other effects come from it. However, I'm going to focus on these three in the book as they are also the easiest to do something about. I recommend working with an endocrinologist in a medical setting only. Not trying to fix your hormones on your own.

There are a few neurotransmitters we need to be aware of because these are key in how we feel on a day-to-day basis. They are:

1. Dopamine: Associated with reward, motivation, and pleasure. Dysregulation of dopamine is linked to conditions like Parkinson's disease and schizophrenia.
2. Serotonin: Regulates mood, appetite, and sleep. Imbalances in serotonin levels are connected to mood disorders like depression and anxiety.

Dopamine

Dopamine is a pivotal neurotransmitter with a multifaceted role in the brain. Operating through binding to specific receptors on neurons, it influences various critical functions, spanning from motivation and reward processing to motor control, mood regulation, attention, learning, and more.

At its core, dopamine is a key player in the brain's reward system. When pleasurable experiences occur, such as savoring a delightful meal or receiving positive feedback, dopamine is released in areas like the nucleus accumbens. This release reinforces behaviors linked to these positive experiences, driving the brain to seek similar occurrences in the future.

There are three main aspects to rewards:

1. Pleasure: This is a significant part of what makes a reward feel rewarding. When we encounter something pleasurable, like tasting delicious food or experiencing something enjoyable, our brain releases chemicals like dopamine that make us feel good. This pleasure reinforces our desire to seek out similar experiences in the future.

2. Learning: Rewards are also closely tied to learning. Our brains are wired to associate actions with outcomes. For example, if we do something that leads to a positive outcome (a reward), our brain remembers this and encourages us to repeat that action in the future. This is known as conditioning, where we learn to associate certain actions with rewards.

3. Motivation to Act: Rewards not only make us feel good but also drive us to take action. Think about how you might work hard to earn money or study diligently for good grades – these actions are motivated by the promise of a reward at the end. Rewards create a sense of motivation that compels us to pursue them.

Dopamine holds significant sway over motor control and coordination. The relationship is evident in Parkinson's disease, where the loss of dopamine-producing neurons in the substantia nigra leads to motor symptoms like tremors and rigidity.

Not limited to the reward and motor domains, dopamine substantially impacts mood and emotion regulation. Fluctuations in dopamine levels are implicated in mood disorders such as depression and bipolar disorder. Certain drugs can modify dopamine activity, potentially ameliorating mood-related symptoms.

Dopamine also shapes cognitive processes, like attention and learning. By modulating the significance of stimuli, dopamine helps direct attention to pertinent information while filtering out less relevant inputs. Dysregulation of dopamine is tied to conditions like attention deficit hyperactivity disorder (ADHD).

The neurotransmitter's role extends to addiction as well. Its involvement in the brain's reward pathways contributes to addictive behaviors, as drugs of abuse can elevate dopamine levels, intensifying pleasure sensations.

Schizophrenia, too, is linked to dopamine imbalance. The "dopamine hypothesis" suggests that excessive dopamine activity in certain brain regions contributes to positive symptoms like hallucinations and delusions.

Think of dopamine like a messenger in a company. Imagine you're in charge of a team that's working on a project. Whenever your team accomplishes a task or achieves a goal, you send a positive message to everyone in the team. This message serves as recognition and encouragement for their hard work.

Similarly, in the brain, dopamine acts as a messenger that delivers a "good job" signal when something positive happens. When you experience something rewarding or pleasurable, your brain releases dopamine, which tells your brain that what you just did or experienced was a good thing. This helps reinforce your brain's desire to repeat those actions in the future, just like your team would want to continue doing good work to receive those positive messages from you.

So, just like your encouraging messages motivate your team to keep working hard, dopamine motivates your brain to seek out positive experiences and repeat behaviors that lead to rewards.

Serotonin

Serotonin, a neurotransmitter, holds a pivotal role in regulating brain and bodily functions. Known as the "feel-good" neurotransmitter, it significantly influences mood, emotions, and overall well-being.

A key function of serotonin lies in mood regulation. It's integral to managing feelings of happiness, emotional equilibrium, and contentment. Imbalances are associated with mood disorders like depression and anxiety, influencing emotional processing and responses to stress and fear.

Moreover, serotonin's engagement in sleep regulation and the body's internal clock underscores its role in sleep-wake cycles. It's a precursor to melatonin, a hormone governing sleep patterns.

Serotonin's influence extends to appetite and digestion. It helps modulate hunger and satiety sensations, affecting appetite control and weight. In the realm of cognition, it has implications for memory and learning, correlating with cognitive performance.

Its role in pain perception and processing highlights its significance in the central nervous system. Some antidepressants that target serotonin levels are also employed to manage chronic pain conditions.

Despite its association with positive emotions, serotonin's role is intricate, and imbalances can have diverse effects on mental and physical health. The equilibrium of serotonin levels is vital for overall well-being and optimal brain performance.

Imagine serotonin as a conductor of emotions in your brain orchestra. Just like a conductor guides the music's mood and tempo, serotonin directs your emotional harmony. When the conductor (serotonin) is skilled and well-balanced, the music (your emotions) flows smoothly, creating a beautiful symphony of positivity and contentment.

In this analogy, low levels of serotonin are like a conductor missing cues, leading to discordant notes and mood imbalances. On the other hand, when the conductor is in control and guiding emotions effectively, the emotional performance is uplifting and balanced.

Much like a conductor's influence extends beyond the music, serotonin's impact reaches various aspects of your well-being, from mood and emotions to sleep patterns and even appetite. Just as a skilled conductor ensures a captivating musical experience, maintaining balanced serotonin levels contributes to your overall emotional harmony and mental health.

Other Notable Neurotransmitters

Acetylcholine: Involved in muscle control, memory, and attention. It plays a crucial role in the neuromuscular junction and cognitive processes.

GABA (Gamma-Aminobutyric Acid): Acts as a major inhibitory neurotransmitter, regulating brain activity by reducing neuronal excitability. It's important for maintaining a balance between excitation and inhibition.

Glutamate: Serves as the primary excitatory neurotransmitter, promoting neuronal activity. It's essential for learning, memory, and overall brain function.

Now that we've discussed the neurotransmitters that play a role in brain function we'll now look at the first official hormone on the list; testosterone.

Testosterone

Testosterone, a fundamental sex hormone found in both males and females, significantly impacts multiple aspects of human physiology, extending beyond its conventional reproductive role. It notably affects brain function, energy levels, and the capacity to pursue and achieve goals.

As a man in the US specifically, it's instilled in us to want to have high levels of testosterone. Popular culture, social media and the current state of our social landscape showcase men with higher levels of testosterone as more masculine; which they are in the physical sense such as more muscle, a deeper voice and more facial hair. Beyond its portrayal in movies and memes, testosterone, found in both men and women, holds the keys to brain function, energy levels, and the relentless pursuit of goals. What we're missing as a culture is the biological part of why having normal testosterone levels is good. And men's testosterone levels are dropping over the decades at the same ages. Low testosterone levels pose challenges. Cognitive functions may decline, making it hard to focus on tasks. Diminished energy disrupts both physical vigor and mental vitality, hindering sustained efforts toward goal attainment.

The study, "Secular decline in male testosterone and sex hormone binding globulin serum levels in Danish population surveys" by Andersson and team, investigated age-independent trends in male serum testosterone levels. Analyzing samples from Danish population surveys conducted between 1982 and 2001, researchers found that serum testosterone decreased and sex hormone binding globulin (SHBG) increased with age. Notably, there were also significant trends in testosterone and SHBG levels over time, indicating lower levels in more recently born men. These changes were not solely due to age, as adjustments for factors like BMI influenced the results. Essentially, men's testosterone levels are at lower levels at the same age as their counterparts in earlier decades.

This is a problem because testosterone plays such a vital role in our mood and energy levels. Lower levels of testosterone have been shown to cause depression.

This meta-analysis, "Association of Testosterone Treatment With Alleviation of Depressive Symptoms in Men: A Systematic Review and Meta-analysis" by Walther and team, focuses on the potential of testosterone treatment as an alternative or supplementary option for countering depressive disorders in men. Antidepressants are commonly used but show limited effects. The study aimed to determine if testosterone treatment could alleviate depressive symptoms in men and the factors that might influence its effectiveness.

The analysis of 1,890 men indicated that testosterone treatment was associated with a notable reduction in depressive symptoms compared to placebo. The effectiveness was quantified, showing odds of improvement, and the acceptability was also assessed.

Overall, testosterone treatment shows promise in reducing depressive symptoms in men, especially when using higher dosages and selecting appropriate samples. If you've ever had depression you know that it feels like your world is foggy. And if it gets worse you may start to judge yourself for feeling foggy and depressed, thus further pushing you into depression. It may be less of a "character flaw" or other harsh terms our brains might box us in as and more of a biological result of hormone levels.

Testosterone contributes to goal-driven behavior. Adequate levels result in higher energy, stamina, and enthusiasm for both physical and mental activities, boosting the drive to overcome challenges. It enhances motivation for pursuing objectives, encouraging individuals to set ambitious goals and display determined effort toward their realization.

Its interaction with dopamine is intriguing. Elevated testosterone levels amplify the brain's response to dopamine, heightening the sense of reward and motivation. This dynamic relationship forms a feedback loop, where goal pursuit triggers dopamine release, intensifying the motivation to persist.

BIG Note: I'm not saying everyone should go and take testosterone. This is laying the groundwork for why we may be experiencing brain fog, which would be due to low testosterone. Nowhere in the research does it show higher levels of testosterone equate to higher levels of focus or IQ. So please don't take this as a green light to do anything stupid. Check with an endocrinologist first before assuming anything about your hormone levels.

When I got that first blood draw back on my testosterone levels at 25 years old I was shocked. It came back at 220 ng/dL. Which is considered ground-floor low for a man in his mid-20s. That number should've read around 600 to 800 ng/dL to be more normal for my age at that time.

I'm a bit of an odd case though because I just went through testicular cancer, chemotherapy and the roughest few years of my life ever. But when I saw that it had more of an emotional impact on me than I thought. Because testosterone is so glorified in our culture I felt sub-par, like I wasn't good enough at that time. I know it's just a biological marker but that's how it felt to me. It makes sense now looking back at it because I felt AWFUL.

Today, my testosterone is over double and continues to rise with each new method I employ in my lifestyle. I'm working with an endocrinologist and visit him multiple times a year to check in on my T Levels. Here's the thing, I'm not taking any testosterone or medications to directly improve my testosterone levels. I'm only taking thyroid medications because those levels were super low too. By proxy, my testosterone levels have risen dramatically from several things, notable mentions are improved nutrition, gut and sleep. But one of the biggest players in increasing my testosterone is improving my thyroid function. Again, because I had low levels in the first place. This is a different situation for someone with normal levels.

My mood is better, energy levels higher and my ability to have sustained focus throughout the day massively increased. Testosterone isn't a magic bean that'll help us sprout wings but if our levels are out of whack we sure do need to get them to normal levels. Now, speaking of those thyroid levels, let's dive into why that matters for everything else.

Thyroid

The thyroid, the head coach, the Nick Fury of the hormone world, the destroyer of worlds and the maker of life. The thyroid plays such a big role in every part of the body yet many of us don't know it's power. It's like the One Ring, if you don't know what it does it just seems ordinary. Specifically, it's impact on the brain is 'power overwhelming', affecting mood, cognition, and neurotransmitter activity, to name a few.

Thyroid hormones, mainly triiodothyronine (T3) and thyroxine (T4) are produced by the thyroid gland located in the neck. When the thyroid gland is functioning optimally, it releases these hormones into the bloodstream in appropriate amounts to support the body's needs. However, when there's an imbalance, such as in conditions like hypothyroidism (underactive thyroid) or hyperthyroidism (overactive thyroid), it can result in a variety of neurological and psychological symptoms.

Focus and cognition are highly influenced by thyroid function. When thyroid hormone levels are too low, as in hypothyroidism, individuals may experience symptoms like brain fog, difficulty concentrating, and memory issues. This is partly because thyroid hormones are essential for the synthesis of proteins and phospholipids in the brain, which are critical for neuron function and interneuronal communication.

Thyroid hormones, especially T3, help produce certain brain proteins. T3 binds to neuron receptors, affecting protein production. A lack of thyroid hormones decreases protein creation, impacting neuron function.

This upcoming analogy uses references from the Star Wars universe. I'm a big Star Wars nut so if you're unfamiliar with Star Wars, don't worry! The main idea is to understand the relationships between the different components in a fun and fictional context.

In the vast galaxy of your brain, proteins are like the countless Jedi Knights, skilled and essential for keeping peace and order. Each Jedi, from those mastering the Force to the ones building lightsabers, has a distinct role, ensuring that the galaxy operates harmoniously.

Now, the thyroid hormones, especially our notable ally T3, can be likened to the Jedi Council. The Council oversees the training and deployment of Jedi Knights. When T3 is in abundance and functioning well, it's as if Master Yoda himself is guiding the Jedi, ensuring that there are enough of them, well-trained and ready for their roles. But if the Force— or in this case, the thyroid hormones— is disturbed or weak, it might mean fewer Jedi Knights are trained. The galaxy then becomes vulnerable, with sectors unguarded and tasks unfinished.

Diving deeper into our analogy, the brain cell's outer layer, made of phospholipids, is akin to a Jedi's lightsaber. If it's well-constructed, a Jedi can block, fight, and win battles with utmost precision.

Again, our trusty Jedi Council (the thyroid hormones) plays a role here. They ensure that lightsabers are crafted perfectly. Without their guidance, a Jedi might wield a flawed lightsaber, making it harder to face challenges or even communicate with fellow Jedi.

To sum it up, for the galaxy of our brain to remain in balance, we need both skilled Jedi Knights (proteins) and top-notch lightsabers (cell membranes). The Jedi Council, or the thyroid hormones, oversees this balance. Disturbances in the Force, or imbalances in these hormones, might plunge the galaxy into chaos, affecting the brain's overall functionality. May the Force be with your brain!

Energy levels are also closely tied to thyroid function as well. Thyroid hormones play a significant role in cellular metabolism. When the body doesn't have enough of these hormones, cellular activities slow down, leading to feelings of fatigue and lethargy. On the other hand, an overactive thyroid can cause increased metabolism, making an individual feel restless or anxious.

Dopamine also has a relationship with thyroid hormones. While the exact mechanism isn't fully understood, thyroid hormones can influence dopamine levels in the brain. Hypothyroidism may lead to decreased dopamine receptor sensitivity, making it harder for individuals to experience pleasure or motivation. This can further lead to symptoms like depression and apathy.

As for testosterone, while it's primarily associated with the reproductive system, it has indirect interactions with thyroid function. Thyroid hormones can influence the metabolism of sex hormones like testosterone. Low thyroid levels can sometimes lead to low testosterone levels in men, leading to symptoms like reduced libido, fatigue, and mood disturbances. Conversely, high levels of thyroid hormones can increase the metabolism of testosterone, potentially decreasing its overall effect in the body.

The exact cause of brain fog in the context of thyroid dysfunction is multifactorial. It's likely a combination of reduced metabolic activity in brain cells, imbalances in neurotransmitters, and alterations in blood flow and energy utilization in the brain.

All of these play a role in the importance of getting the thyroid levels balanced to have healthy neurotransmitters operating in the brain.

Cortisol

In my first week at the first job I had out of college in San Francisco, in 2013, I experienced a new level of mental fatigue that I hadn't felt in some time. It was in the afternoon on that first Thursday. I needed to speak with different people and project manage the sales pipeline. As I was typing in an Excel spreadsheet and my mind blanked out on what I had done before. I was feeling very stressed the entire week and I had already made multiple mistakes and beaten myself up about it.

As I'm trying to think about this spreadsheet I cannot recall which sales I had already gone over. It was wild and I'd never felt that before but I knew it wasn't good. My mind wasn't supposed to be missing beats and dropping information on the same day. This was one of my most impactful brush-ups with a cortisol rush I'd ever felt. I wish it was a one-off that day but I experienced that week after week at that job for over a year. It wasn't until years later that I learned how to keep myself calm and relaxed in situations like that through breathwork, mindfulness and other biohacks shared later in this book.

Cortisol, a pivotal steroid hormone, is the adrenal glands' answer to stress. Earning its nickname, the "stress hormone", cortisol is released in greater quantities during moments of heightened tension, especially when the body's fight-or-flight reflex is activated. While its primary role is to galvanize the body to respond to immediate threats—by mobilizing energy, altering immune responses, and sharpening senses—it also casts a more prolonged shadow over some of our brain's most vital functions, notably memory.

After an experience, memories undergo a process of consolidation to be stored for the long term. Elevated cortisol levels, especially if they're sustained, can impair this consolidation process. Consequently, while you might vividly recall an event shortly after it happened, its details might become hazy as time goes on. Similarly, high cortisol can impede the retrieval of memories, making it challenging to recall information even if it is successfully stored.

The hippocampus, a seahorse-shaped structure deep within the brain, is a linchpin in memory formation and retrieval. Prolonged exposure to elevated cortisol can disrupt the delicate neural architecture of the hippocampus, diminishing its capacity to form and recall memories. Over time, this could lead to significant memory deficits.

Stress and elevated cortisol can tilt the scales of memory, making negative experiences more concrete. This means that under chronic stress, individuals might recall negative memories more readily than neutral or positive ones, which can further perpetuate feelings of anxiety or sadness. Which can disturb serotonin and dopamine levels over time. Leading to more depression or increased anxiety levels.

Serotonin governs a spectrum of functions beyond just mood. Its equilibrium can be disrupted under the shadow of chronic stress. Elevated cortisol levels, a marker of prolonged stress, can alter serotonin receptors and its synaptic availability. Such a disruption skews the brain's serotonin balance, and an inadequacy here is associated with mood afflictions like depression.

Parallelly, dopamine, as a reminder, plays pivotal roles in motivation, motor control, mood regulation, and attention. Yet, this system isn't impervious to cortisol's influence. Heightened cortisol can impact the dopaminergic system, affecting dopamine release and receptor sensitivity. This imbalance can usher in issues ranging from depression and attenuated motivation to attention deficits.

We'll go more into what to do to keep stress levels low in part two. But it's good to know that acute moments of stress and chronic stress can impede our brain power so that we can do something about it in the future. This leads us to the next troll, Mentropy Troll. This stands for "Mental Entropy," which is around our thoughts going into chaos and how that increases stress levels.

Mentropy Troll: Mental Entropy - Thoughts Moving To Chaos

Entropy is a concept that arises in various disciplines, most notably in thermodynamics and information theory. I first heard about it when I began researching physics in college.

I'm fascinated by the universe, the cosmic world and what's beyond our solar system. And at a point in college I was exploring other majors that I could go into. I dabbled in learning more about the universe and was talking about it with my dad. He then pulled out a book called Entropy that had been passed down through our family. It wasn't a hugely significant book but just something that we had around.

As I looked through it I quickly realized I didn't want to be a physicist! That jumble was beyond what interested me because it went into details I couldn't care less about. But I learned what entropy was and it's always stuck with me because I find it such a catch-all term that be applied to multiple situations.

Entropy, in thermodynamics, is a measure of the amount of energy in a system that is unavailable to do work. It's often also described as a measure of the disorder or randomness of a system. The second law of thermodynamics states that in any energy transfer or transformation, the total entropy of a closed system will always increase over time, approaching a maximum value.

The concept of entropy was first introduced in the context of thermodynamics in the mid-19th century. The primary figure associated with its discovery is the German physicist Rudolf Clausius.

In the 1850s and 1860s, Clausius formulated the second law of thermodynamics and introduced the concept of entropy as a way to describe the amount of thermal energy in a system that could not be used to perform mechanical work. His work helped clarify the distinction between energy that can be utilized for work and energy that cannot, which is essentially the core idea behind entropy in thermodynamics.

Think of entropy as a measure of how mixed up or scattered energy is within a system. The more mixed or random the energy is, the higher the entropy.

Imagine a room, and if clothes are neatly folded and arranged, it has low entropy (orderly). If clothes are scattered everywhere, it has high entropy (disordered).

In this context, entropy is about unpredictability. If you flip a perfect coin, you can't predict whether it'll be heads or tails – it has high entropy. If you have a rigged coin that always lands heads, there's no unpredictability (or surprise) – it has low entropy.

In both cases, entropy can be thought of as a way to measure how "spread out" or "unpredictable" things are.

Imagine you have a cup of hot coffee in a cold room. Initially, the coffee is much hotter than the room (so there's an "order" to it – hot coffee, cold room). Over time, if you just leave it, the heat from the coffee will spread to the room, and the coffee will cool down. Eventually, the temperature difference disappears, and everything reaches a sort of "middle" temperature. The energy from the coffee has dispersed or spread out. This is an increase in entropy – the system has moved from order (distinct hot and cold zones) to a sort of "chaos" (everything lukewarm).

These can be likened to the increasing "temperature" of the mental system. Just as a physical system may be more prone to disorder when "heated" or under external pressures, our mind under stress is more susceptible to chaotic, high-entropy states. Anxious and ruminative thoughts can spread, just as heat spreads in a room, making everything feel 'warmer' or more stressful.

As everything becomes more stressful our thoughts may become more catastrophic. This is a cognitive distortion where the mind jumps to the worst possible outcomes. It's akin to a system jumping to a state of maximum disorder with a minor trigger. If our mental system is already prone to high entropy (e.g., we're already anxious or stressed), then a small event can lead to a disproportionate cascade of negative thoughts, similar to how a small nudge can lead to a big mess if a room is already in a precarious state.

Mental entropy is a less formalized concept than entropy in thermodynamics or information theory, but it can be a useful metaphor for understanding the state of our minds. The Mentropy Troll deals with our psychology, thoughts and internal state of mind as it impacts our physical biology.

Just as physical systems tend to drift towards disorder if not actively maintained, our minds can drift into chaotic and unproductive patterns if not actively managed. This can be understood as an increase in "mental entropy." It's important to understand why our minds do this. And you've most likely heard all this before but it's worth mentioning again because it really explains why our minds lean towards the negative.

Early humans faced numerous life-threatening challenges, from predators to intra-species conflicts. For survival, it was more advantageous for our ancestors to remember and focus on negative experiences (like a near encounter with a lion) than positive ones (like finding a tasty fruit). Remembering that lion could save your life the next time, but forgetting a fruit source, while not optimal, wasn't immediately life-threatening. This tendency to give more weight to negative experiences is termed "negativity bias." Over countless generations, the brains that were best at detecting, reacting to, and remembering these threats were the ones that survived and reproduced.

Imagine your mind as a garden. When nurtured, pruned, and attended to regularly, it remains orderly, and flowers bloom. But if left unattended, weeds might grow, overshadowing or choking out the flowers. In the same way, if we don't actively manage our thoughts, they can become overrun with negativity, anxiety, and rumination.

Using the garden metaphor, the "weeds" can be likened to these automatic negative or anxious thoughts. They sprout easily (because of our evolutionary history) and can be quick to take over if not addressed. Evolution "designed" these weeds to grow fast because they had a survival advantage.

Our modern environment is vastly different from the ancestral environment that shaped our brains. Many of the threats our ancestors faced are no longer present, yet our brains are still wired to detect and react to threats.

To thrive in the modern world, we need to actively attend to our mental garden. This means recognizing these evolutionary-rooted tendencies and using various strategies to manage or counteract them.

In essence, our brains have been shaped by evolution to be on guard and to prioritize negative information. This was adaptive for our ancestors but can be maladaptive in many modern contexts. Just as a garden can be overrun by weeds if not cared for, our minds can be dominated by these evolutionary-rooted negative patterns if we don't actively address them. So how does this affect brain fog?

If you think of cognitive clarity as flowers in our mental garden, stress is like a large, overshadowing tree that sprouts suddenly. It blocks sunlight and diverts nutrients, making it harder for the flowers (clear thoughts) to thrive.

While acute stress might have helped our ancestors avoid immediate threats (like predators), chronic stress wasn't as typical in ancestral environments as it is today. Chronic stress can lead to constant activation of the stress response, putting us into a more sympathetic dominant state, which is not what our body was designed for.

In our garden analogy, if the large overshadowing tree (stress) doesn't get uprooted and stays for too long, the flowers are continuously deprived, leading to a garden full of shadows or "brain fog."

Chronic stress results in sustained elevated levels of the hormone cortisol; as we discussed earlier. This can be likened to the soil in our garden becoming less fertile over time due to the persistent overshadowing and nutrient diversion.

Chronic stress can also lead to rumination, where individuals constantly turn over worries in their minds. This rumination can become a source of stress itself, forming a feedback loop. Such repeated negative thought patterns can further intensify brain fog.
The garden equivalent would be if the weeds (negative thoughts) not only grew fast but also released seeds that led to even more weeds, taking over more and more space.

During my time in San Francisco, I dealt with this chronic stress daily. At work, I'd have to be putting out corporate fires. At the end of each month, I'd be running around chasing sales reps down to manage the sales pipeline and make sure nothing got lost. If I missed reporting one of those deals it could've been thousands of dollars missed in our calculations. So I felt the pressure of that environment when I wasn't really ready or that committed to it.

Now, don't get me wrong. I excel in high-stakes environments with lofty expectations; in fact, I often flourish. However, the caveat is that I need to be passionate about the task. The root of my dilemma in San Francisco was a lack of genuine enthusiasm for the job and an absence of deep-seated passion for the company. This isn't to imply that my colleagues felt the same; many were quite dedicated and found their true calling there. But for me, it wasn't the right fit.

Because of this, plus the added pressure of sales, I experienced chronic mental stress for 18 months. I didn't feel good, my brain felt fried every day and I felt like that kid from Jurassic Park who got an electric shock by holding onto the dinosaur fence.

My thoughts weren't rooted in empowering energy either. I'd get bitter, cynical, fearful, and anxious. My thoughts ranged from, "Oh I made another mistake, damnit! I can't do anything right."

At other times, I'd feel an acidic feeling inside and seeth with rage. Thinking something like, "Why does this sales rep always pester me with such demands, and with such a bad attitude?"

At my lowest, insecurity would creep in: "They probably don't appreciate me here. What if they let me go? How will I manage my bills? I barely have savings to last a few weeks. Would I need to relocate, branded as a failure?"

These are the thoughts that if left unattended can run wild in one's own mind. They will slowly spread their sticky, lingering darkness and take root as a parasitic mushroom taking over its prey; reminiscent of the insidious nature of the cordyceps mushroom species.

David Goggins, a former Navy Seal, author and speaker on becoming a tougher human, once said, "Only you can master your mind, which is what it takes to live a bold life filled with accomplishments most people consider beyond their capability." If you're unfamiliar with Goggins, I highly recommend diving into his book "Can't Hurt Me" once you've finished with this one. He offers profound insights on leveraging hard work and adversity to build mental strength.

This is what we're talking about, building up mental resilience so that the mind doesn't take over. It's vital to work through pain and reduce stress simultaneously. The balance of exercise and recovery is the same dance.

When managing your mind and thoughts just remember this. You are the observer and ultimate decision-maker of what thoughts flourish and hold power. You cannot control every thought that pops into your head but you can decide whether or not to dwell on it. Or to dwell on more empowering and invigorating thoughts.

By understanding the relationship between chronic stress and brain fog in both evolutionary and metaphorical terms, we can appreciate the need to address and manage stress. We'll be discussing in further depth, in part two, what to do to destress and manage one's thoughts.

Cave Troll: Physical Inactivity

You know some people who really know how to unwind and binge-watch their favorite streaming shows? I've come across a few who truly master the art of relaxation. And while I absolutely enjoy my fair share of video games and catching up on the latest series (The Bear, Ted Lasso, rewatching Modern Family) they seem to have a special talent for it. The Cave Troll is when we get caught in bouts of physical inactivity and a lack of exercise. And I definitely fall into that cave from time to time!

The issue is when there's not enough exercise happening in this situation. Working as a personal trainer, I've encountered individuals who haven't engaged in structured exercise for extended periods. They often approach me with various physical discomforts and concerns about weight gain, mentioning decreased productivity and energy levels. I deeply understand and empathize with their circumstances. It's heartening to see them taking proactive steps towards better health. From there, we begin their journey slowly, often starting with tools like fitness bands, TRX support straps, and basic bodyweight exercises to establish a foundational strength.

In 2018, I was in a bad head-on car collision. The driver swerved into my lane coming around a tight corner. I remember trying to turn away but they smashed right into me. I remember the car coming at me but I blacked out during the collision. I came to it in my car sitting on the shoulder of the road. I remember people coming up to the other driver's car and then coming to me. I couldn't open my door, because it was smashed in, so I had to crawl out of the window.

A woman walking by who saw the incident came up to me and said, "Hey that was a horrible accident, you should really lay down until the paramedics get here. You know know what injuries you could've sustained."

I said, "I'm fine, I'm just a little cold."

It was chilly out but this was also Florida. At that moment I didn't feel any pain and I felt like someone gave me the biggest adrenaline shot ever. I'd never been so mentally lit in my life. It was like I was in the zone at the Olympics or something. My mind had given me clarity and presence.

I called my girlfriend at the time, now my wife. We were going to a Trevor Noah comedy show in Tampa, Florida that Sunday evening with some friends. I told her about what happened and she immediately started heading in my direction.

The ambulance arrived and put me in a neck brace and stretcher for precautionary purposes. As I slid into the ambulance, we made our way to the hospital. I didn't have anything broken but later I'd find out about the permanent neck damage, bulged discs, herniated lower back, busted knees, bruised ribs, and crushed nose.

I was grateful that it wasn't worse. But for 6 months after that accident, I couldn't do much physical exercise. I was always the athletic type, so this was hard for me. Emotionally, not just physically. I wanted to pump iron and lift weights but after a few feeble attempts, I knew that wasn't going to happen.

So I did my three days a week chiropractic visits and physical therapy sessions. I also walked as much as I could. But I remember during that time I wasn't able to get in quality exercise. My mood was down, my mind mush, and my spirits low. Eventually, I was able to get my strength back. I started with bodyweight training and got to a point where I could do a few pull-ups again.

Because of that experience, I can relate to people when they have body pains or haven't worked out in some time. It's hard at first but once you get into the swing of things it gets easier.

Okay, let's dive into some uncomfortable areas to see why physical inactivity is potentially adding to brain fog. It's good to educate ourselves on the "what if negative" side of situations so we can know what we're dealing with.

Physical activity promotes blood circulation throughout the body, including the brain. Regular exercise ensures that the brain receives adequate oxygen and nutrients delivered via the bloodstream. When you're inactive, there may be reduced blood flow to the brain, which can lead to decreased cognitive function and the feeling of "fogginess."

Reduced blood flow can affect various cognitive functions, from short-term memory to attention span. Tasks that once seemed easy might become challenging due to the sluggish supply of oxygen and nutrients to the brain.

Blood circulation doesn't just supply the brain with what it needs; it also helps remove waste products. Inactivity and decreased blood flow mean that metabolic byproducts accumulate, potentially harming neurons and contributing to the sensation of brain fog. Over time, chronic inactivity and the associated reduced cerebral blood flow can increase the risk of cognitive decline and neurodegenerative diseases.

Also, exercise helps in the release of neurotransmitters such as serotonin, dopamine, and norepinephrine. These chemicals play a role in mood regulation, motivation, and cognitive clarity. Physical inactivity can lead to an imbalance or decreased production of these neurotransmitters, potentially contributing to feelings of brain fog, depression, or anxiety.

Physical activity prompts an immediate release of neurotransmitters. This is partly why people often feel a "high" or an uplifted mood after a workout. The term "runner's high" refers to the euphoric feeling runners sometimes get after an extended period of activity, which is believed to be due to a combination of neurotransmitter release and endorphin production.

Regular exercise not only causes a short-term boost in neurotransmitter levels but can also increase the overall availability and sensitivity of these chemicals in the brain over time. This effect can act as a protective factor against mood disorders and cognitive decline.

Reduced levels or imbalances in neurotransmitters can cloud one's ability to think clearly, leading to a feeling commonly referred to as "brain fog." This sensation involves feelings of confusion, forgetfulness, and a lack of focus and mental clarity.

Chronic physical inactivity can lower the levels of these critical neurotransmitters, increasing the risk of mood disorders such as depression and anxiety. This is why exercise is often recommended as an adjunctive treatment for these conditions. With dopamine being central to motivation, decreased production due to inactivity can lead to feelings of apathy and reduced drive to engage in activities.

In addition, physical activity helps regulate sleep patterns. A consistent exercise routine can promote deeper, more restful sleep, which is vital for cognitive function and clearing brain fog. Physical inactivity, on the other hand, can disrupt sleep patterns, contributing to fatigue and reduced mental clarity.

And exercise acts as a natural stress reliever by reducing the levels of stress hormones like cortisol. Without regular physical activity, stress can accumulate, and chronic elevated stress is known to contribute to brain fog.

Later in the book, in part two, we'll look at different kinds of exercise to do to optimize health and brain power.

I've played sports and exercised for most of my life. Baseball, hockey and weight training in my younger years. Soccer, obstacle courses, weight lifting, and endurance running in my adult years. I can't go a week without doing some kind of exercise, besides the recovery time after the car accident, or else my body's energy levels dip by a significant amount and my mood dries up into a toasted marshmallow. Once you have the exercise bug it gets you like a great video game will suck you in. Now, speaking of heavy breathing let's look at the next troll. The Oxy Troll.

Oxy Troll: Low Oxygen Levels

In the bustling city of Cellville, numerous factories diligently produced energy known as ATP, relying on raw materials from the distant Oxygenia, transported by blue trucks. As these factories operated, they produced a waste byproduct, carbon dioxide, which was managed by a fleet of red trucks. One day, disruptions halted the blue trucks from Oxygenia, causing a decline in ATP production, a dimming of lights and a darkening of the mood in the city.

Simultaneously, the red trucks faced challenges, leading to an accumulation of waste in Cellville. Recognizing the crisis, Cellville's governing council implemented strategies to restore efficient transport and waste management. With these measures, Cellville returned to its optimal function, embodying the critical balance of intake and elimination in biological systems.

The tale of Cellville underscores the criticality of balance for optimal function, mirroring how our bodies operate. In the context of our physiological systems, oxygen acts as the essential "raw material" delivered to our cellular "factories." When there's a disruption in oxygen supply, akin to the blue trucks in Cellville not delivering efficiently, our cells can't produce the required energy (ATP) efficiently.

Just as the dimming lights of Cellville represented a city operating below its potential, reduced oxygen levels in our bodies mean our cells can't function at peak capacity. This deficiency in cellular energy production manifests as fatigue, both physically and mentally. We become the embodiment of the dimmed Cellville, operating in a low-energy state.

Therefore, the story of Cellville reinforces the idea that just as a city needs consistent raw materials to thrive, our bodies need a steady supply of oxygen to maintain energy and ward off fatigue. If this balance is compromised, the entire system feels the repercussions.

While it might seem subtle on the surface, poor breathing habits can indeed cause significant disruption to our body's functioning.

Breathing is our primary means of delivering oxygen to the bloodstream and removing carbon dioxide. Even minor disturbances in this process can affect cellular function. Cells rely on oxygen for energy production. A consistent reduction in oxygen availability means cells have to work harder to produce the same amount of energy or produce less energy overall, leading to feelings of fatigue.

Our breathing patterns can influence the balance between our sympathetic (fight or flight) and parasympathetic (rest and digest) nervous systems. Chronic shallow breathing can keep the body in a sympathetic dominant state, leading to chronic stress and its associated negative effects.

This ties into our earlier Trolls as they relate to chronic stress which can lead to Mental Entropy or chaotic, anxious, or damaging thoughts. If we're too much in the sympathetic dominant state then our body's not getting the chance to relax, rebuild and recover. All of this can then also create elevated levels of cortisol hormone. Which, as we saw in earlier chapters, can cause brain fog, memory issues and an overall cognitive decline.

This poor breathing which exacerbates the sympathetic nervous system can lead to digestive processes being inhibited, potentially leading to issues like indigestion, bloating, or other gastrointestinal problems. Thus causing the gut-brain axis, Tummy Troll, to become imbalanced.

The brain is particularly sensitive to changes in oxygen and CO_2 levels. Suboptimal oxygen delivery can impact cognitive functions, including attention, memory, and decision-making. Simultaneously, an accumulation of CO_2 can dilate blood vessels in the brain, potentially leading to headaches and further cognitive disruptions. For example, have you ever seen in movies or shows where the characters have a low-oxygen situation? They get loopy and don't seem to have their full cognitive function.

Over time, chronic poor breathing can contribute to or exacerbate health issues such as sleep apnea, cardiovascular problems, and metabolic disorders.

While for many people, the effects of suboptimal breathing might not be immediately noticeable or dramatic, the long-term cumulative impact can be significant. It's akin to driving a car with a slightly misaligned wheel; it might not seem like a big deal on a short journey, but over a cross-country trip, the wear and tear on the vehicle can be substantial.

That said, it's also important to note that while poor breathing habits can contribute to health issues, they are just one piece of a complex puzzle comprised of the other Trolls we've discussed so far. Low oxygen and poor breathing habits is probably lower on the list of brain fog causes but when you're doing everything else right, it may be the last key to the door of clarity. Think of it as a chain of dominos; if you've already aligned and set most of them right, the last few can make a considerable difference in achieving the desired outcome.

After the car accident I was in, my nose got deviated and became visibly misaligned. Breathing has become harder and harder to get enough oxygen through my nostrils. I'm working with an ENT (ear, nose, throat) doctor now to discuss surgery to fix my deviated septum and open up my nostrils.

But in the meantime, I've been wearing nasal strips that keep my nose slightly more open at night. That small shift has helped me get much better sleep. My brain is getting more oxygen for the seven to nine hours I'm asleep. In the morning I feel more alert and rested than not wearing the nasal strips.

Also, when my gut starts flaring and acting up it puts inward pressure on my lungs. And deep breathing becomes more difficult for me because of the tightness in my chest and belly region. I have to force my stomach out and bring my chest up to get a full breath of air when my gut's acting up. This is also why it's important to get the gut healthier.

While we should all have our noses checked to be sure they've not deviated, you don't have to have a deviated septum to feel the effects of low oxygen. By performing chest breathing instead of belly breathing our breaths can become more shallow. Therefore, getting less oxygen in each inhale.

So be aware of how you're breathing. Hold your hand on your belly and be sure to take slow, deep, and paced-out breaths. Holding a good posture will help you get in full breaths of air as well. Did you just sit up more in your chair? Me too! Now, let's move on to the next and final Troll which probably has the biggest impact on brain fog on a day-to-day basis, sleep.

Pillow Troll: Chronic Poor Sleep

I think it goes without saying that when you don't get a good night's sleep you feel lethargic, brain foggy and out of it the next day. I put it last because, well, it's the most obvious but this Troll probably has the biggest impact on our cognition on a day-to-day basis.

Poor sleep acts as a cognitive disruptor, muddying the clarity of our thoughts and hampering our ability to concentrate. When the brain is deprived of its essential restorative periods, neural pathways can become less efficient, leading to a lack of focus on any given task. As a result, tasks that usually seem straightforward become challenging, and maintaining focus on any one activity becomes an uphill battle.

Sleep deprivation primarily affects the prefrontal cortex, the brain region responsible for executive functions such as decision-making, problem-solving, and most importantly, attention. When this area is compromised due to lack of sleep, our cognitive bandwidth narrows. It becomes increasingly challenging to filter out distractions, prioritize tasks, or even hold onto a single thought for an extended period.

Sleep is not merely a passive state of rest for the body; it is an active period of restoration and regulation for the brain. One of the pivotal processes that occur during sleep is the regulation of neurotransmitter levels and their receptor sensitivities. There are three main neurotransmitters sleep affects, serotonin, dopamine and norepinephrine; which should be becoming more familiar to you at this point.

An imbalance in serotonin levels can lead to mood disorders, sleep disturbances, and a host of other physiological and psychological issues. Proper sleep ensures optimal dopamine release, which is critical for maintaining motivation, attention, and motor coordination. And norepinephrine acts as both a hormone and a messenger in the brain. It's involved in the body's stress response, alertness, and attention. When we are sleep-deprived, norepinephrine levels can become irregular, potentially leading to heightened stress and poor attention.

Lack of sleep can heighten our stress response, primarily through erratic norepinephrine activity, making us more reactive and less patient.

Neurotransmitter imbalances affect not only our emotions but also our cognitive abilities. Memory, attention span, decision-making, and problem-solving can all suffer when neurotransmitter levels are off-kilter. Speaking of memory, what topic was next?

Memory

Memory consolidation is one of the brain's pivotal functions during sleep. When we talk about memory, we often picture it as a straightforward storage system, like saving a file on a computer. In reality, the process is more intricate and dynamic, especially during our sleeping hours.

During the day, our brains are constantly bombarded with information, both trivial and significant. This data is temporarily stored. Come nighttime, and during certain stages of deep sleep, the brain starts the process of sifting through this reservoir of information. Essential data, the experiences and learnings we need for the long term, are methodically transferred and integrated into long-term memories. This process is termed "consolidation."

However, when our sleep cycles are interrupted or cut short, this consolidation process is hampered. The information that remains in the short-term storage, which is not designed for long-term storage, can become jumbled or even discarded. This disruption is similar to a computer not being given the time to save a file properly. The result is gaps in our memory or the sensation of information being "just out of reach."

This memory lapse isn't just about forgetting names or misplacing items. It can lead to brain fog. The disruption in memory consolidation, induced by poor sleep, can make it hard for individuals to draw upon past experiences or knowledge effectively. In situations requiring quick thinking or decisive action, this can limit one's ability to make a good call.

Stress Levels Rise

When we're consistently deprived of sleep, our body perceives it as a threat, prompting a series of defense mechanisms. One primary response is the increased secretion of cortisol, as we've discussed previously, often labeled the "stress hormone."

Cortisol, typically peaks in the early morning, providing a wake-up jolt to kickstart our day, and diminishes as the day progresses, reaching its lowest during the night. However, with sleep deprivation, this pattern becomes dysregulated, leading to elevated cortisol levels throughout the day and even into the night.

The brain becomes persistently alert. While this heightened alertness might sound advantageous, it's the kind akin to a car's alarm system being too sensitive—reacting even to a gentle breeze. This hyper-vigilance means our brain is continuously on the lookout for potential issues, even when they don't exist. Such a state can be exhausting and makes focusing on a single task challenging. The brain becomes more prone to distractions, seeing them as potential "threats" or "alerts" that need immediate attention.

With heightened cortisol levels, individuals tend to be more emotionally reactive. A minor inconvenience can trigger disproportionate irritability or frustration. This emotional volatility can further reduce our patience threshold, making sustained focus on tasks more difficult, as we're more likely to be interrupted by our emotional responses.

Beyond just cognitive disruptions, elevated cortisol can lead to a cascade of physical symptoms like increased heart rate, higher blood pressure, and muscle tension. These physical manifestations can create a feedback loop, where the body feels perpetually "on edge," reinforcing feelings of stress and anxiety. These all add to our previously mentioned sympathetic states which have a cascade of effects downstream.

The knowledge of being sleep-deprived and the palpable effects it has on one's cognition can create another feedback loop. One might become anxious about their performance due to lack of sleep, which in turn elevates stress levels, making quality sleep even more elusive.

In a broader sense, the body's stress response, when activated continuously due to lack of sleep, doesn't just derail our immediate focus; it reshapes our cognitive landscape. It creates a mental environment where concentrating on tasks becomes an endeavor, not just because of immediate distractions but due to a persistent undercurrent of stress and the body's constant state of high alert.

I don't know about you but I, unfortunately, can't function well on sleep under about eight solid hours. It's hard because that means I really have to prioritize sleep and be in bed about nine hours before I need to wake up. Sometimes I'm not even tired nine hours before bed but once I start laying down my body gets the hint and goes into relaxation mode, and then I slowly drift off.

There are some people who truly function on less sleep. And as jealous as I am of those types I realize that's not me. I don't play that game, I stick to what I know I need.

Arnold Swarzenneger once said he only gets six hours of sleep and his jovial advice to people is to just "sleep faster." As funny as that is, not everyone can operate like that. He is also a genetic freak of nature and could probably recover quicker than about 99 percent of the human race. He was also on performance-enhancing drugs which helped him recover quicker than the average Joe. I love Arnold and his story but I definitely disagree with his advice for everyone to sleep six hours. It matters most on your specific body type, genetics, exercise intensity and how you're recovering for how many hours you need. But most people need more than less.

In the next section, we'll be going into the top brain hacks for now dealing with the seven Trolls of brain fog we've discussed. We have gone deep into the problems now let's explore solutions. Some of these are old school with new variations and others truly cutting edge in our modern world. As we're ending on sleep, this is also where we'll be slumbering onto first in the brain hacks next.

Part Two

In the book's initial section, I introduced the 7 Trolls of Brain Fog, which, from my research and experience, are the predominant culprits behind the cloudiness of the mind.

Moving on to the second part, I'll unveil 44 actionable brain biohacks that can revitalize your cognitive abilities. I've personally tried all of these at some point, with many becoming staples in my daily routine. While I encourage exploring these strategies, I don't anticipate you to embrace all immediately. It's about finding what resonates with you and tailoring it to your needs.

When we engage with a book, it's not about absorbing everything but cherry-picking the nuggets of wisdom that align with our journey. My hope is that you'll discover a few brain biohacks that intrigue you, and over time, discern their transformative potential.

Beyond the universally acknowledged trio of sleep, exercise, and wholesome nutrition, my standout techniques for enhancing brain power include fasting, exploring nootropics, and tuning into focus-enhancing music during tasks. However, the crown jewel lies in mind hack #29: the pursuit of inner peace. Okay, let's get to it diving head first into the sheets.

Pillow Paradise

In the first part of the book we looked at the seven Trolls of brain fog. We ended last with sleep because it's the most obvious but also the most important. Because of its importance, that's where we're starting with first in the brain hacks section.

As we discussed, adequate sleep is important for physical, cognitive, and emotional health, and is critical for maintaining a healthy immune system, improving memory consolidation, and regulating mood and emotions.

In our house, sleep is sacred. My wife and I have a rule that if the other person is sleeping we try our best to not disturb them. We also give ourselves ample time in bed for lag time: which is the time it takes for the brain to finally shut down. For example, if I go to bed at 9:30 pm I may not fall asleep until 10:00 pm because I'm just thinking about things.

I always try to get good sleep because I feel like crap and have horrible productivity the day after a poor night's rest. Speaking of which, let's dive into what I've found works for getting good sleep. Starting with how to deal with those ruminating thoughts.

#1: Daytime Sleep Disturbances

In a study done by Akerstedt and his team called "Sleep disturbances, work stress and work hours: a cross-sectional study", they studied how work stress, work hours, and other lifestyle factors can affect sleep.

They surveyed 5720 healthy people with jobs in Stockholm. The results showed that people who had a lot of work demands and physically hard jobs had a higher chance of having troubled sleep. On the other hand, people who had strong social support at work had a lower chance of having sleep problems.

Overall, the study found that stress from work and our social environment can significantly affect our sleep. It also showed that being unable to stop worrying about work during free time can be a major factor affecting sleep.

There are a few key pieces to this study that I find interesting. The first part is that it mentions people who have strong social support have a lower chance of experiencing sleeping problems. That goes to show the importance of relationships in our life.

Another point is that the physical demands of a job also play a significant role in sleep disturbances. This underscores the importance of ergonomics and the physical well-being of employees in the workplace. Proper job design and considerations for physical tasks can possibly lead to better sleep for employees.

Additionally, the fact that those who are unable to detach from work concerns during their off-hours experience more sleep issues highlights the importance of work-life balance. It's essential for individuals to have mechanisms to mentally switch off from work-related worries during their personal time. This could involve engaging in relaxation techniques, hobbies, or other activities that divert the mind from work-related stresses.

Furthermore, while the study doesn't dive deep into the specifics of how many hours of work led to sleep disturbances, it does hint at the broader theme of overwork and its relation to sleep quality.

Overworking, or the so-called "burnout", has become a prominent issue in many modern societies. It would be interesting to see if there's a threshold of working hours beyond which sleep disturbances become more prevalent.

Overall, this study highlights the intricate relationships between work, social support, physical demands, and sleep quality. As the lines between work and personal life continue to blur, especially in our digital age, it is essential for us to disconnect from work and cool down to relax when it comes time to sleep.

The most actionable item here is to not be doing work-related projects or mentally demanding tasks within an hour or so before bed. That way it gives our brain time to wind down. Constantly thinking about work or mentally demanding tasks can keep the brain in a heightened state of alertness.

By setting a boundary and allowing time to detach, we help the brain transition from a state of high activity to relaxation. When we engage in work-related tasks or mentally demanding activities, there's a risk of becoming fixated on problems or challenges. This rumination can extend into our bedtime, making it harder to fall asleep. Taking a break can reduce the chances of such rumination.

This is the biggest helper for me. To do a purely relaxing activity within an hour before bed. That could be watching a show, doing a hobby with my hands or stretching with breathwork. I've lately been into leatherworking. This is a great hobby because I can get lost in the doing of it with my hands. It gets me out of my head and gives me something else to focus on in a relaxing way. Finding activities like this can help build in some of that buffer time to get the brain to chill out before sleep.

#2: Limit blue light before sleeping

Have you seen those orange-lensed glasses going around on all the biohacker's faces lately?

Those are blue light-blocking glasses. They're aimed at limiting blue light to the eye to help with sleep.

Blue light is a type of light that is emitted by electronic devices such as smart phones, tablets, and computers. Exposure to blue light can disrupt the body's natural sleep-wake cycle by suppressing the production of melatonin, a hormone that helps regulate sleep.

Studies have shown that exposure to blue light before bedtime can delay the onset of sleep, reduce the amount of time spent in deep sleep, and result in less restorative sleep overall. This sleep disruption can lead to daytime drowsiness, mood changes, and difficulty concentrating.

One study by Shechter, et al. 2017, took 15 participants comprised of men and women and had them wear blue light-blocking glasses or non-blue light-blocking glasses for 2 hours before bed for 1 week.

They found that wearing blue light-blocking glasses preceding bedtime for 1 week improved sleep in individuals with insomnia symptoms.

Furthermore, it's not just the sleep-wake cycle that's affected by blue light. Extended exposure can also potentially contribute to digital eye strain, which is characterized by symptoms like dry eyes, blurred vision, and headaches. This phenomenon arises from prolonged screen usage without adequate breaks, with blue light being a significant contributing factor.

Aside from glasses, there are other strategies people employ to reduce blue light exposure:

- Screen Filters: Many devices now come with settings that reduce blue light emissions in the evenings. Features like Apple's "Night Shift" or Android's "Night Mode" adjust screen colors to warmer hues after sunset.
- Apps: There are dedicated apps available for computers and phones that reduce blue light based on the time of day.
- Limit Screen Time: This is perhaps the most straightforward method – simply reduce the amount of time spent in front of screens during the evening.

I tried wearing blue light-blocking glasses for a while but I didn't like wearing them after a while. So I use the iPhone's blue light setting in the phone to automatically turn on from 6 pm to 5 am. And I make sure to not scroll or use my phone much within about two hours of sleep. Sometimes I get caught in but mostly I stick to that rule and it's served me well.

To minimize the negative effects of blue light on sleep, it's best to keep blue light limited to up to 2 hours before bedtime.

#3: Keep it cold

If you've ever woken up in the middle of the night with the sheets sticking to your legs because you're sweaty then you'll deeply understand this section.

Keeping the temperature turned down at night, between 66 and 73 degrees Fahrenheit, could help you get better sleep for a few reasons.

A cooler room temperature can promote deeper, more restful sleep. This is because a cooler environment slows down metabolic processes and decreases brain activity, making it easier for the body to enter into a deep, restorative sleep.

Additionally, cooler temperatures can help regulate the production of melatonin, a hormone that plays a key role in regulating sleep-wake cycles.

Our body temperature naturally drops as we fall asleep, and a cooler room temperature can help facilitate this process. When the body is too warm, it can be difficult to fall asleep and stay asleep. Additionally, a cooler environment can help reduce the risk of disruptions caused by night sweats or discomfort due to overheating.

Sleep-related disorders such as insomnia and sleep apnea can be exacerbated by an uncomfortable sleeping environment. By keeping your bedroom cool and comfortable, you can reduce the risk of these and other sleep-related disorders. Additionally, a cooler sleeping environment can help reduce the risk of snoring, which can be disruptive to both you and your sleeping partner.

I live in Florida, and it gets as hot as a dragon's breath after eating spicy tacos! So I have to be extra sure that I keep cooler at night, especially during the summer. I have my thermostat on an automatic schedule so that I don't have to think about it. And since the air can sometimes take a while to cool down to the temperature I want, with the automatic schedule it's always ready when I go into bed. Usually about an hour before I plan to go to sleep I have my thermostat schedule turned to 72 degrees Fahrenheit. I've found this to be the sweet spot in my home.

While cold does help us sleep better, another reason why it's better to keep it cold is because heat can cause wakefulness and decrease slow-wave sleep and rapid eye movement sleep. Essentially, a lack of heat helps us sleep better too - which means crank it down!

Bonus tips for keeping it cool and comfy:

- Use breathable bedding materials such as cotton or linen
- Consider investing in a mattress that promotes airflow and heat regulation. Or get a mattress that has cooling built in. There are more and more coming onto the market now. Eight Sleep is one brand that's doing a good job.

#4: Keep it dark

This one may seem obvious but if you don't wake up with the sun then you'll want to invest in blackout curtains. It's been a game-changer for me. I sometimes wake up around 5:30 am but on other days I want to sleep in I need that light gone.

This also means no TV in the room shining blue light everywhere.

There are several reasons why keeping it dark in a bedroom can help us get better sleep:

Melatonin is a hormone that regulates our sleep-wake cycles. It's produced by the pineal gland in the brain in response to darkness and is inhibited by light. By keeping your bedroom dark, you can help your body produce more melatonin, which can help regulate your sleep and promote deeper, more restful sleep.

Light can disrupt our sleep, even if it's just a small amount. Exposure to light during the night can suppress the production of melatonin and interfere with our natural sleep-wake cycles. This can lead to difficulty falling asleep, more frequent awakenings during the night, and overall lower sleep quality. By keeping your bedroom dark, you can reduce the risk of these disruptions and promote more restful, restorative sleep.

Our circadian rhythm is our body's internal clock that regulates many of our physiological processes, including sleep. Light exposure during the night can interfere with our circadian rhythm, making it more difficult to fall asleep and stay asleep. By keeping your bedroom dark, you can support your body's natural circadian rhythm and promote better sleep quality.

#5: Create a nightly routine

Getting a good night's sleep is essential for maintaining good health and well-being. However, many people struggle to get the sleep they need due to stress, anxiety, and other factors. One way to improve your sleep is to create a nightly routine that promotes relaxation and helps you wind down after a long day.

Many people experience stress and anxiety that can make it difficult to fall asleep. By incorporating relaxation techniques into your nightly routine, you can help calm your mind and reduce stress, making it easier to fall asleep.

A nightly routine can help establish a consistent sleep schedule, making it easier to fall asleep and wake up at the same time each day. This can help regulate your body's internal clock and improve the quality of your sleep.

A nightly routine can help promote relaxation and calmness, which can make it easier to fall asleep and improve the overall quality of your sleep. Relaxation techniques such as deep breathing, meditation, or stretching can help you unwind and prepare for sleep.

My nightly routine:

It's the same every night so I get into a habit of it and then start to get tired because it's my habit trigger for sleep:

1. Drink magnesium water (for gut and muscle relaxation)
2. Take vitamin C and a magnesium supplement (for gut and muscle relaxation)
3. Stop drinking water 30 minutes before bed, to not have to pee as badly at 3 am
4. At a certain time, my air conditioning cooling turns on. I scheduled it to turn to 69 degrees Fahrenheit every night, so if I forget I'm not going to bed hot.
5. The blue light blocking schedule is also on my cell phone, turning on at 7 pm
6. No work or deep thinking an hour before bed.
7. Watching a light and fun streaming show to keep my mood up and my mind distracted but not too engaged an hour before bed
8. No playing on my cell phone 30 minutes before bed to not activate my mind too much
9. 10 minutes before bed: Brush teeth
10. 8 minutes before bed: Wear a nose breather strip to help me get more oxygen when I sleep. My nose is slightly deviated (will probably get surgery on it eventually). This has helped me get a higher quality of sleep because I'm getting more oxygen.
11. 6 minutes before bed: Take two quick inhales followed by a slow exhale, three times. To put the body into a parasympathetic relaxation state.
12. 3 minutes before bed: Gratitude prayer.
13. Sleep time: Dog set in her bed, wife set on her side of the bed and lights off.

Tips for Creating a Nightly Routine

Here are some tips for creating a nightly routine that promotes relaxation and better sleep:

Establish a consistent bedtime:

Try to go to bed and wake up at the same time every day, even on weekends. This can help regulate your body's internal clock and improve the quality of your sleep.

Create a relaxing environment:
Make your bedroom a sleep-conducive environment by reducing noise, lowering the temperature, and eliminating distractions such as electronic devices.

Incorporate relaxation techniques:
Try relaxation techniques such as deep breathing, meditation, or yoga to help you unwind and relax before bed.

Limit caffeine and alcohol:
Avoid caffeine and alcohol before bedtime, as they can interfere with sleep quality and make it more difficult to fall asleep. I have a rule not to drink caffeine after 3 pm because it could still be in my system around bedtime. For alcohol, if I drink I'll have my last drink at least 3 to 4 hours before bedtime, if possible.

This is because it'll give your body time to process the alcohol and allow your body to recover in sleep instead of cleaning up the alcohol in your liver. For example, if I have a few drinks at dinner around 6 pm I'll stop around 7 pm and then go to sleep around 10:30/11 pm.

#6: Make the room only for sleep and romance

Our minds understand the physical surroundings we're in often quicker and more in-depth than we do. It calculates millions of bits of information from the walls, the scratches on the fan, the color of the foot of the bed and how the air conditioner is moving the curtains.

Our minds also understand that certain physical environments and rooms we're in hold emotional and psychological history, for each person.

I don't mean if you're in the Roman Coliseum you're mind knows all the fights. I mean if you always relax and stream shows in your living room your mind knows that space is for relaxing.

The same goes for your bedroom. If you have a computer set up in your bedroom and do work or play video games in there your mind will acknowledge that space for focus/play mode. Then when you go to sleep, your mind thinks you're in the work or play space and it won't be able to relax as easily.

So if you keep your bedroom for sleep, sex and maybe meditation before sleeping you'll find it's easier to get into a state of sleepiness when winding down for bed.

#7: Avoid stimulating activities

I've mentioned this a few times now but it deserves its own bucket here because it's that important. Avoid activities that can be stimulating or stressful before bedtime, such as work-related tasks or engaging in vigorous exercise. I typically do nothing work-related or anything that requires me to engage in deep thought within an hour before bed.

Stimulating activities can keep your mind amped up and ready to go! It may also keep your nervous system in a more sympathetic state, which is the fight or flight response state, instead of the relaxed parasympathetic state.

The sympathetic and parasympathetic nervous systems are two branches of the autonomic nervous system that work together to regulate many physiological processes in the body, including the release of hormones. The sympathetic nervous system is responsible for the "fight or flight" response, which prepares the body for stressful or challenging situations, while the parasympathetic nervous system is responsible for the "rest and digest" response, which promotes relaxation and recovery.

Some hormones are more closely associated with the sympathetic nervous system, while others are more closely associated with the parasympathetic nervous system.

Here are some examples:

Sympathetic Hormones:
- Adrenaline (epinephrine)
- Norepinephrine
- Cortisol (although it can also be released in response to stress by the hypothalamic-pituitary-adrenal axis)
- These hormones are released in response to stress or other stimuli that activate the sympathetic nervous system, and they help prepare the body for action by increasing heart rate, blood pressure, and energy availability.

Parasympathetic Hormones:
- Acetylcholine
- Oxytocin
- Endorphins

These hormones are associated with the parasympathetic nervous system and are released during states of relaxation, pleasure, and social bonding. They can help promote feelings of calm, well-being, and connection with others.

#8: No social media scrolling

Scrolling through social media will keep your brain in impulse and immediate gratification mode.

In the study, "Electronic Device Use before Bedtime and Sleep Quality among University Students" (Pham HT, et al.), they examine the relationship between electronic device use before bedtime and sleep quality among university students.

They found that cell phone use near bedtime for a duration longer than 30 min was associated with poorer sleep quality among university students. Specifically, the study found that students who reported using electronic devices before bed had a higher likelihood of experiencing poor sleep quality, including difficulty falling asleep, difficulty staying asleep, and waking up feeling tired or unrefreshed.

This is definitely something that I've found myself caught in at times. You sit down on your bed, open your phone for a notification and then bam, 20 minutes later you're still scrolling through the feed. Dangit! Got me again.

That's why it's important to immediately hook the phone up to its charger and put it face down once you get in your bedroom. You'll feel more at ease and ready to go to sleep.

Nutritious Delight

In this section, you'll either be pleasantly delighted or harshly disappointed. The world of nutrition is currently embroiled in a fierce battle, with various diets like vegan, carnivore, paleo, Mediterranean, pescatarian, and many more vying for the top spot.

Now, I must confess that I do have my personal preferences when it comes to food choices, and I'll certainly share those with you. However, when it comes to the broader population, I firmly believe that there is no one-size-fits-all perfect diet. It's a unique journey for each individual to discover what foods work best for their own body and genetic makeup. It's a journey of finding what foods work best for your body and with your genes. For me, this is what my typical day of eating looks like:

Morning: Fasting. No food since 6 pm or 7 pm the night before. Only water with electrolytes, alpha-gpc, bacopa, L-theanine (you'll learn about why in the upcoming section on nootropics) and black coffee without creamer. It must be this because any calories, especially creamer, will take my body out of a fasted state.

Break–Fast: 12 pm I have a high-protein smoothie with eggs on toast. The smoothie typically has a banana, honey, peanut butter, and two scoops of whey protein resulting in about 60 grams of protein. I'll then eat four eggs on toast, adding another 25 grams of protein. Altogether, with proteins from the other food items, it's about a 90-gram protein "breakfast."

Second meal: at 3 pm I'll then have a second meal. This is usually a sandwich on gluten free bread or a plate of animal protein, carb and veggie. For example, the sandwich I'll due sliced turkey breast with sriracha or a 93 percent ground beef, home cooked, burger. For the plate, I'll do 93 percent ground beef, or ground turkey, or chicken thigh, or fish of some kind with rice/potatoes and broccoli.

Dinner: Then at 6 or 7 pm, depending on my schedule that day, I'll eat my last big meal. It'll usually be something similar to the second meal with a different variation.

Protein dessert: Then after dinner, I'll usually have a non-fat, plain (for low sugars), Greek yogurt with a serving of raisins and lightly sprinkled nuts. Note, that adding too many raisins can make it a sugar bomb.

I've found this combo to give my brain full power. Meaning, total clarity for about the first 8 hours of my day. Then I hit a slight tired lull. Then my energy picks back up giving me a second wind. Then I get tired and wind down for bed. I tried eating breakfast in the morning but it hazes my mind too much. So this seems to be the winning combo. I can go for about 10 to 12 hours of productive time on this schedule before my focus becomes mush.

You'll learn more about fasting in the upcoming section and how to get started with it. But first, one of the biggest things I've found to detract from brain power is processed foods.

#9: Limit processed foods

Behind sleep, nutrition is probably the second most important element for a healthy, energetic, and cognitively optimized body and brain.

What you put in your body you will become. Literally, the foods you eat are broken down and used for parts of your body. Feel your shoulder right now. That was food! The proteins are broken down into amino acids and then your body builds them back up as skin cells, muscle cells, bones, tendons, ligaments, nerves, arteries, veins, and capillaries to form your shoulder. It did this with the how-to manual of your genes through genetic expression.

Pretty rad huh? This is why it's incredibly important to your overall health and cognitive performance to eat the best food possible.

Since you're a dedicated health nut you've probably tried diets and other forms of nutrition before. Maybe you dabbled in keto, paleo, low carb, vegan, carnivore or a myriad of other diets. That's okay, I'm not here to preach about one diet specifically.

For me, right now, I've found a gluten-free, paleo, kind of carnivore diet that works best for my body and gut bacteria. Veggies sometimes give me horrible bloating. So I stick to the meats and fruits mostly.

However, my biggest tip to you for whatever diet you're eating is to limit processed foods!

Of any diet you pick, I guarantee that's a staple requirement of that diet. Now, notice I didn't say *eliminate*, but instead, I said limit.

Because our world right now has such an abundance of processed foods I think it'd be near impossible to eliminate them 100%. Possible? Yes. But it's near impossible to do.

What does 'limit' look like?
It means only 5 to 10 percent of foods you eat are processed.

What Exactly Are Processed Foods?

Processed foods are foods that have been altered in some way from their natural state through the use of various processing techniques such as canning, freezing, drying, baking, and packaging. These foods are typically high in calories, salt, sugar, and unhealthy fats, and are often low in nutrients such as fiber, vitamins, and minerals. Processed foods are typically designed to be convenient, affordable, and have a long shelf life, which makes them popular among consumers.

Examples of processed foods include

- Sugary drinks and soda
- Pre-packaged snacks such as chips, cookies, and candy
- Fast food and fast-casual restaurant meals
- Frozen dinners and meals
- Processed meats such as bacon, sausage, and deli meats
- Canned soups, vegetables, and fruits
- Baked goods such as cakes, pastries, and bread

Processed foods can have a negative impact on health in a number of ways. They can contribute to weight gain, obesity, and other health problems such as type 2 diabetes, high blood pressure, and heart disease. They may also be linked to an increased risk of certain types of cancer.

Most are also high in vegetable oils. This leads us to our next hack.

#10: Limit vegetable oils

Vegetable oils are a type of highly processed oil that is extracted from various plant sources such as soybean, corn, canola, sunflower, and safflower. They are commonly used in cooking and food production because they are inexpensive and have a high smoke point, which means they can be heated to high temperatures without burning.

But why are they ubiquitous in our food products today? And where did they come from?

The Industrial Revolution, which took place during the 18th and 19th centuries, had a profound impact on the production and consumption of vegetable oils worldwide. The introduction of new machinery, innovations in transportation, and increased global trade contributed to the growth and diversification of the vegetable oil industry.

The development of advanced machinery during the Industrial Revolution, such as steam engines and mechanized seed presses, greatly improved the efficiency of vegetable oil production. These innovations allowed for higher yields and faster processing, making vegetable oils more affordable and accessible to a larger consumer base. Additionally, the invention of the continuous screw press in the mid-19th century further streamlined the oil extraction process and reduced the need for manual labor.

The increased demand for vegetable oils led to the cultivation of a wider variety of oilseed crops. In the United States, for example, cottonseed oil became an important byproduct of the booming cotton industry during the 19th century. Similarly, the cultivation of sunflower, soybean, and rapeseed expanded in Europe and North America to meet the growing demand for vegetable oils. The expansion of oilseed crops not only diversified the types of vegetable oils available but also contributed to the growth of agricultural economies in many regions.

The Industrial Revolution facilitated global trade and transportation, allowing for the exchange of goods and ideas between different continents. As a result, vegetable oils such as palm oil from Africa and coconut oil from the Pacific Islands began to be imported and used in Europe and North America. Improved transportation methods, such as steamships and railroads, also made it easier to transport raw materials and finished products, further expanding the reach of vegetable oils and contributing to their widespread adoption in cooking and food production.

During the Industrial Revolution, marketing and advertising played a significant role in shaping consumer preferences and promoting the use of vegetable oils. Companies began to advertise vegetable oils as healthier, more affordable, and more versatile alternatives to traditional animal fats like butter and lard. As a result, the consumption of vegetable oils increased dramatically, and they became a staple ingredient in many households.

Now that we know a little bit about vegetable oil's history, to understand why vegetable oils are harmful it's important to know what the lipid bilayer is.

The lipid bilayer is a structure found in cell membranes that are composed of two layers of phospholipid molecules that form the wall of each individual cell. These phospholipids have hydrophilic (water-loving) heads and hydrophobic (water-fearing) tails, which create a barrier that separates the inside of the cell from the outside environment. The lipid bilayer also contains cholesterol and other lipids that help maintain its integrity and fluidity.

Vegetable oils are a type of fat that can be incorporated into the lipid bilayer of cell membranes. However, the composition of vegetable oils is different from the natural fats found in our body, such as saturated fats and monounsaturated fats. Vegetable oils are typically high in polyunsaturated fatty acids (PUFAs), particularly omega-6 fatty acids, which can be incorporated into the lipid bilayer and alter its properties.

Studies have shown that consuming high amounts of omega-6 fatty acids from vegetable oils can lead to changes in the lipid composition of cell membranes, particularly in the brain. These changes can affect the function and stability of cell membranes, which can have implications for brain health and cognitive function.

Additionally, the high levels of PUFAs in vegetable oils can increase the susceptibility of cell membranes to oxidative damage, which can contribute to inflammation and a range of chronic diseases. This is because PUFAs are more prone to oxidation than saturated and monounsaturated fats, which can lead to the formation of harmful compounds such as free radicals.

However, despite their widespread use, vegetable oils have been linked to a number of health problems, including:

1. High in Omega-6 Fatty Acids: Vegetable oils are typically high in omega-6 fatty acids, which are essential for the body but can be harmful when consumed in excess. Omega-6 fatty acids can promote inflammation in the body, which is linked to a range of health problems such as heart disease, cancer, and arthritis.
2. Low in Nutrients: Vegetable oils are highly processed and often stripped of their nutrients during the extraction process. This means they are low in essential nutrients such as vitamins, minerals, and antioxidants.
3. High in Trans Fats: When vegetable oils are heated, they can undergo a process called hydrogenation, which creates harmful trans fats. The World Health Organization (WHO) has called for global elimination of industrially-produced trans fats by 2023. If that doesn't say enough about trans fats I don't know what will.
4. Can Increase Oxidative Stress: Vegetable oils, especially polyunsaturated ones, are highly susceptible to oxidation, leading to the formation of free radicals. These free radicals can damage cells and contribute to aging, inflammation, and various diseases.
5. Linked to Obesity: Some studies have suggested that consuming vegetable oils may be linked to weight gain and obesity. This is thought to be due to the high-calorie content of these oils and their ability to promote inflammation in the body.

In contrast, consuming healthy fats such as olive oil, butter (yes, full-blown freaking butter!), ghee, and coconut oil may have a range of health benefits. These fats and oils are typically less processed and contain a range of nutrients such as vitamins, minerals, and antioxidants. Choosing healthy fats over vegetable oils can help improve overall health, and cognitive performance and reduce the risk of chronic diseases.

Vegetable oils are commonly used in a wide variety of processed foods, including:

- Margarine
- Mayonnaise
- Salad dressings
- Baked goods such as cookies and cakes
- Fried foods such as french fries and chicken nuggets
- Snack foods such as chips and crackers
- Processed meats such as sausages and deli meats
- Frozen foods such as frozen pizza and frozen dinners
- Non-dairy creamers
- Cooking oils such as soybean oil, corn oil, canola oil, and sunflower oil

#11: Eat more nutritious, whole foods

I hate reading a nutrition book that says "cut out this food" and "don't eat that food group" and it seems like it's more about what not to do than guiding me on what to eat. So, I didn't want to fall into that in my own book.

So, what should we eat? Nutritious, whole foods. For me, I follow mostly a paleo, gluten free, diet which includes a lot of the foods coming up.

Whole foods are unprocessed or minimally processed foods that retain their natural nutrients and fiber. They include fruits, vegetables, poultry, red meat, seafood, and zero-processed starchy carbs. These foods are nutrient-dense, providing essential vitamins, minerals, antioxidants, and healthy fats that support brain health and cognitive function.

Building a Brain-Boosting Diet

To optimize brain function, aim to incorporate a variety of whole foods into your daily diet. Here are some key components:

A) Fruits and Vegetables:

I've found people are often scared of eating fruit because they've been told it's high in sugar. It is mainly sugar but it's not processed sugar, it comes with micronutrients and it has fiber to slow the absorption. You don't have to be scared of eating fruit because berries especially are great for brain health and are low in sugar for the serving.

Fruits and vegetables are rich in vitamins and minerals that are essential for brain health. For example, vitamin C, found in citrus fruits and leafy greens, helps to protect the brain from oxidative stress and may help to improve cognitive function. Similarly, folate, found in leafy greens and legumes, is important for brain development and function.

They're also rich in antioxidants, which help to protect the brain from damage caused by free radicals. Free radicals are unstable molecules that can damage cells and contribute to the development of neurodegenerative diseases, such as Alzheimer's and Parkinson's. Antioxidants like vitamin C, vitamin E, and beta-carotene, found in fruits and vegetables, can help to neutralize free radicals and protect the brain from damage.

They are a good source of fiber, which can help to regulate blood sugar levels and reduce inflammation. Chronic inflammation has been linked to a range of health problems, including cognitive decline and neurodegenerative diseases.

Many fruits and vegetables, such as watermelon and cucumbers, have a high water content, which can help to keep the brain hydrated and functioning properly.

B) Meat and Lean Proteins:
Many people are considering a vegetarian diet because they think meat might be unhealthy. I disagree with this because meat is a wonderful source of protein that you just can't get from a vegetarian diet. Red meat has been linked to heart disease but that's not true. Also, some of those studies use red meat equal to that of a hot dog. Yeah, hot dogs will make you unhealthy. But not organic, free-range ground beef.

Proteins are made up of amino acids, which are the building blocks of neurotransmitters in the brain. Neurotransmitters are chemicals that allow neurons in the brain to communicate with each other. Amino acids like tryptophan, tyrosine, and phenylalanine are essential for the synthesis of neurotransmitters like serotonin, dopamine, and norepinephrine.

Red meat is an excellent source of iron, which is essential for the brain's oxygen supply. Iron is a component of hemoglobin, which carries oxygen to the brain and other parts of the body. A lack of iron can cause anemia, which can lead to cognitive impairment and decreased brain function.

Meat, particularly beef, is a good source of vitamin B12. Vitamin B12 is important for the proper functioning of the nervous system and the formation of red blood cells. A deficiency in vitamin B12 can lead to neurological problems, such as memory loss and depression.

C) Seafood:
Seafood is one of the best dietary sources of omega-3 fatty acids. These fatty acids are important for the development and maintenance of the brain, and they have been shown to improve cognitive function, memory, and mood. Omega-3 fatty acids are also anti-inflammatory,

which can help to protect the brain from damage caused by inflammation.

It's also a good source of protein, which is important for the development and repair of brain tissue. Protein is made up of amino acids, which are the building blocks of neurotransmitters, the chemicals that allow neurons in the brain to communicate with each other.

It's rich in minerals like zinc, iron, and selenium, which are important for brain health. Zinc is important for the development and function of the brain, while iron is essential for the transport of oxygen to the brain. Selenium is an antioxidant that can help to protect the brain from damage.

Fatty fish like salmon and mackerel are also good sources of vitamin D, which is important for brain health. Vitamin D plays a role in the development and maintenance of the nervous system, and a deficiency in vitamin D has been linked to cognitive impairment and an increased risk of neurodegenerative diseases.

My favorite is pairing lean seafood with fattier seafood. So that I can get in my protein count without going super high in calories from the fish's fat content. For example, 5 ounces of shrimp with 4 ounces of salmon.

D) Zero-processed starchy carbs:
Zero-processed starchy carbs, such as rice, quinoa, beans, and root vegetables (potatoes), are good for the brain because they provide a steady supply of glucose, which is the brain's primary source of energy. This steady supply of glucose helps to maintain cognitive function and prevent fatigue.

Side note: These are not whole grains or wheat flour-type foods as these can be extremely inflammatory and disruptive to our gut lining.

They're also a good source of fiber, which can help to regulate blood sugar levels and reduce inflammation. Chronic inflammation has been linked to cognitive decline and neurodegenerative diseases.

Root vegetables and rice are good sources of minerals like magnesium and potassium, which are important for brain health. Magnesium is involved in the regulation of neurotransmitters and can help to reduce anxiety and depression. Potassium is important for the transmission of nerve impulses and the regulation of blood pressure.

I eat mostly rice and russet potatoes for this category. I find those don't agitate my gut as much as beans can. Also, they're easy to make in bulk and I find them the tastiest.

8 Great Foods For Brain Health

I know people want to know so I've included specific foods that have been shown to be good for brain health. I don't eat all of these every day but I'll typically have all of these on a monthly basis at least but most weekly. Especially the beef hearts...mmmm!

#12: Fatty Fish

Omega-3 fatty acids, particularly EPA (eicosapentaenoic acid) and DHA (docosahexaenoic acid), have attracted significant attention in the world of nutrition and health. Fatty fish, like salmon, sardines, and mackerel, serve as nature's powerhouse for these nutrients.

The human brain is approximately 60% fat. DHA, one of the primary types of omega-3s, is the most prevalent fatty acid in the brain. It plays a pivotal role in constructing cell membranes in the neurons. Neurons are the primary cells in our nervous system, transmitting information throughout our body. When DHA is available in ample amounts, it ensures that these cell membranes remain fluid and function optimally.

Chronic inflammation is often linked to numerous health problems, including cognitive decline. Omega-3s, especially EPA, have powerful anti-inflammatory properties. By reducing inflammation in the brain, these fatty acids may protect against damage that can lead to cognitive issues.

Beyond cognitive function, there's emerging evidence that omega-3s might play a role in mood regulation and mental health. Low levels of omega-3s have been associated with mood disorders like depression. The anti-inflammatory properties of these fatty acids may help alleviate symptoms by reducing inflammation in the brain, which some studies suggest might be linked to depressive disorders.

#13: Blueberries

Blueberries are a nutritional powerhouse, brimming with antioxidants and flavonoids that shield the brain from potential harm caused by oxidative stress and inflammation. These small yet mighty berries have been the focus of numerous studies, and the findings are compelling. Regular consumption of blueberries has been linked to enhancements in memory, learning capacity, and other cognitive functions.

This can be attributed to their rich content of protective compounds that foster neural connections and brain health. Additionally, the antioxidants present in blueberries play a pivotal role in staving off the cognitive decline typically associated with aging, helping maintain a sharp mind even in later years. So, incorporating these berries into one's diet not only offers a burst of flavor but also a boost to brain health.

Blueberries are one of my favorite fruits. What's nice about blueberries too is that you can eat a lot for the amount of calories and sugar in them. It's a high-volume, low-calorie food. This is useful for adding to meals to give them a sugary zing. I like doing Greek yogurt, low fat and low sugar, with blueberries in it. It's a nice sweet, high-protein, dessert that won't expand the waistline.

#14: Avocado

Avocado, often celebrated as a superfood, is brimming with monounsaturated fats that play a vital role in brain health. These beneficial fats promote optimal blood flow to the brain, ensuring that our cognitive machinery receives the nutrients and oxygen it needs to function effectively.

Beyond just ensuring a steady flow of blood, the monounsaturated fats in avocados also strengthen the integrity of brain cell membranes, acting as guardians to these essential cells. This combination of enhanced blood flow and fortified cell membranes results in a more agile brain, characterized by sharper focus, improved memory, and heightened cognitive performance. So, when you slice open that creamy avocado, know that you're not only indulging in a delicious treat but also fueling a sharper, more alert mind.

But do watch out because these suckers are loaded with fat; one avocado can have 30g of fat! Yes, good fat but don't go throwing back one to two a day or else you'll go throwing back your belts because you'll need bigger ones soon.

#15: Dark Chocolate

Dark chocolate, beyond its indulgent taste, is a treasure trove of flavonoids, potent antioxidants that shield the brain from the ravages of oxidative stress and inflammation. This protective barrier, forged by regular consumption of dark chocolate, offers a myriad of cognitive benefits.

Research has illuminated the positive impact of these rich compounds on brain health, highlighting improvements in cognitive function and mood elevation. Furthermore, there's intriguing evidence to suggest that these benefits aren't fleeting; the antioxidants in dark chocolate might play a role in warding off age-related cognitive decline. Thus, savoring a piece of dark chocolate not only satiates the palate but also offers a boost to the brain, keeping it sharp and vibrant.

Some people worry about the calories of eating dark chocolate daily. While you don't want to overconsume it, generally one serving or less seems to be okay. Depending on your goals and how many avocados you eat daily! But really, dark chocolate shouldn't expand the waistline if everything else is done right. It's usually the quantity that gets people.

#16: Broccoli

Broccoli, often a staple on dinner plates, is more than just a green vegetable; it's a reservoir of essential nutrients that play pivotal roles in brain health. Rich in vitamin K, It contributes significantly to enhanced brain function and memory preservation. But that's not all. Broccoli's glucosinolates, when broken down, transform into powerful compounds known for their anti-inflammatory effects. These compounds diligently guard the brain against the detrimental impacts of oxidative stress and inflammation, ensuring it functions optimally.

And there's a muscle connection too. Broccoli is loaded with agents that reduce myostatin, a protein that can inhibit muscle growth. By keeping myostatin in check, these agents aid muscle development, making broccoli an unsung hero in the diet of many bodybuilders. So, the classic bodybuilder's meal of broccoli, chicken, and rice isn't just about physique; it's a testament to the comprehensive health benefits of this cruciferous marvel.

I love me some broccoli but wow it does not always sit well with my gut. Calling all passengers because this train's going "toot toot."

#17: Eggs

Eggs, often crowned as nature's multivitamin, are teeming with nutrients paramount for brain health, with choline leading the charge. This essential nutrient is the building block for the neurotransmitter acetylcholine, a vital messenger molecule that plays a central role in memory, learning, and an array of cognitive functions.

Thus, incorporating sufficient choline into one's diet translates to improved memory and sharper cognitive abilities. However, the virtues of eggs don't stop at the brain. They're a nutrient-dense package, boasting not only healthy fats that nourish our brain cells but also a substantial protein punch. Contrary to some dietary myths, eggs, especially when paired with gluten-free bread, make for a balanced and nutritious start to the day.

Further enhancing their nutritional profile, eggs contain fortitropin, a compound that aids muscle-building, making them a favorite among fitness enthusiasts and a testament to their multifaceted health benefits.

I love slamming eggs on gluten-free bread, with one slice of pepperjack cheese split between them after a good morning workout. It's so satisfying and knowing they're one of the best muscle builders makes me happy. I also don't feel sluggish after eating them so that only keeps enhancing my focus for the day.

#18: Tomatoes

Tomatoes, often celebrated for their vibrant hue and culinary versatility, are a trove of essential nutrients with profound implications for brain health. Their standout component, lycopene, is a robust antioxidant that serves as a protective shield, safeguarding brain cells from potential harm caused by oxidative stress.

But the benefits of tomatoes don't end with lycopene. They're also packed with vitamin C, a multifaceted nutrient that bolsters brain function in two key ways: by neutralizing free radicals as an antioxidant and by fostering the synthesis of neurotransmitters, the brain's communication molecules. Thus, incorporating tomatoes into one's diet not only adds a splash of color to meals but also offers a substantial boost to cognitive well-being.

I'll eat a fat-boy tomato raw with a little salt sprinkled on. I know some people can't stand them, like my dad - he won't touch it. These add a great wet essence to an otherwise dry dish. I'm talking about you, chicken breast!

#19: Beef Heart

Beef heart, often overlooked in conventional culinary circles, is a nutritional gem packed with Coenzyme Q10 (CoQ10). This compound isn't just any antioxidant; it's a dynamic molecule that guards cells, especially brain cells, against the wear and tear imposed by oxidative damage. The benefits of CoQ10 extend further, with research linking it to enhanced cognitive function and a potential protective role against the onset of neurodegenerative diseases.

I know it sounds disturbing but they're the best-tasting of all the beef organs. Just cook it stove top with butter, salt, and pepper with a good sear. I've been addicted to them lately, give it a shot!

Moving The Meat Sack

This section will highlight different types of exercise you can do to get yourself going that enhance the brain. If you're just starting out or haven't exercised in a while remember to go slow with yourself. I've worked with a lot of people who want to hit the pedal to the metal their first week. Usually, when I'm working with them I can slow them down. However, I don't have that luxury with you right now as you're reading this. So, slow it down, you'll get there but you'll get there a lot slower if you get injured or burnt out too quickly.

#20: Aerobic Exercise

Aerobic exercise is one of the most beneficial forms of physical activity for the brain. When you engage in aerobic exercises, such as running, swimming, or cycling, your heart rate increases and blood flow to the brain is enhanced. This increase in blood flow helps to deliver more oxygen and nutrients to brain cells, which can promote their health and function.

In addition to increased blood flow, aerobic exercise also triggers the release of growth factors in the brain, such as brain-derived neurotrophic factor (BDNF). BDNF is a protein that promotes the growth and survival of brain cells and supports the formation of new neural connections. By increasing the levels of BDNF in the brain, aerobic exercise can help to promote brain health and function.

Research has shown that regular aerobic exercise can have a significant impact on cognitive function. Studies have found that it can improve memory, attention, and executive function, which are important skills for success in both work and personal life. It has also been linked to a reduced risk of age-related cognitive decline and neurodegenerative diseases such as Alzheimer's disease.

This can be a 20-minute bike ride 2 to 3 times a week. Or a run at a low pace, 11/min mile, 2 to 3 times a week. Also, if you make these activities social, you'll get in your relationship-building time and exercise simultaneously. Call a friend to go kayaking. Go cycling with your buddy. Or join a running community club. Whatever it is, you can combine socializing with it to make it more fun and so that you stick with it longer.

I make sure to get in a run or walk at least once a day. Right now I'm training to get better at running for various races so I'm doing this more and more these days. But even walks help me out too.

While aerobic exercise is particularly beneficial for the brain, it's important to note that other forms of physical activity, such as strength training, can also have a positive impact.

#21: Strength Training

While aerobic exercise is often touted as the gold standard for improving brain health and function, strength training can also offer significant benefits for the brain. I'd rather lift weights than run any day. I just like it better but I know cardio is necessary so I do it.

In addition to improving physical strength and mobility, strength training has been linked to improved cognitive function, increased energy levels, and reduced feelings of fatigue and exhaustion.

When I mention strength training I'm talking about lifting weights, moving barbells, doing body weight training and repping on dumbbells.

This means pushing yourself to get stronger with resistance training. I've seen everyone from 5-year-olds to 95-year-olds engage in strength training and I firmly believe that it's good for everyone to do.

One study published in the journal Frontiers in Neuroscience found that strength training improved cognitive function in older adults, including memory and attention. This is because strength training increases blood flow to the brain, which helps to deliver more oxygen and nutrients to brain cells. This increased blood flow can promote brain health and function, and may even help to protect against age-related cognitive decline.

Another systematic review of studies published in the American Academy of Neurology found that engaging in a minimum of 52 hours of exercise is linked to enhanced cognitive abilities in older individuals, regardless of their cognitive status. This suggests that strength training may be particularly beneficial for individuals who are at risk of age-related cognitive decline.

In addition to improving cognitive function, strength training has also been linked to increased energy levels and reduced feelings of fatigue and exhaustion.

Incorporating strength training into your exercise routine can have significant benefits for your brain health, function, energy, and cognition. By taking care of your body, you can support your cognitive function and promote lifelong brain health.

This isn't something I'm going to go into depth within this book but I've been working as a personal trainer and strength coach for years. So if you want help with that reach out to me and I can set you up for a specific program.

Starting out, I'd recommend going with 3 days a week of strength training doing either full body on all the days or doing a push, pull, legs split (PPL). PPL is essentially splitting the 3 workouts into a push day of chest/tricep/shoulder, a pull day of back/bicep, and a legs day.

My coaching clients love involving these types of strength training workouts in their weekly lives. They can see the weights going up and feel them getting easier to lift. They see their muscles growing and their confidence booming. Strength training is a win for a person for its psychological benefits as much as its physiological benefits.

#22: Slow exercises like walking, easy bike riding, and hiking

Walks, slow bike rides and hiking are excellent ways to mobilize triglycerides (fat) out of your adipose tissue (fat cells), get blood flow to the brain and keep the body active without overdoing it.

You wouldn't want to only do this type of exercise because the body does need other forms of exercise such as strength training to fully function. However, don't ignore this kind of exercise because it seems insignificant.

Studies have shown that these forms of exercise can improve cognitive function, reduce feelings of stress and anxiety, and improve overall mood. Additionally, walking has been shown to reduce feelings of stress and anxiety, which can help to improve overall mood and mental well-being.

Similarly, slow cycling has been shown to have positive effects on cognitive function and mental health. A study published in PLoS One found that slow cycling improved cognitive function and reduced feelings of stress. This suggests that even gentle forms of aerobic exercise like slow cycling can have significant benefits for brain health and function.

Incorporating slower forms of exercise like walking, slow cycling, and hiking into your routine can have significant benefits for your brain health, function, energy, and cognition.

A simple rule to follow here is getting 10,000 steps 4 to 5 days a week. Break out a podcast, or audiobook or talk to a friend so you're not bored on the walks.

Stress Management

Stress can have a significant impact on the brain and cognition. When we experience stress, our bodies activate the fight or flight response, which releases stress hormones like cortisol and adrenaline. As we discussed earlier in the Endo Troll, these hormones help us respond to immediate threats by increasing heart rate, respiration, and blood pressure.

However, when stress becomes chronic, it can have negative effects on the brain and cognition. Chronic stress can cause the hippocampus, a brain region involved in memory and learning, to shrink in size. This can lead to memory problems and difficulty learning new information.

Stress can also impair executive function, which refers to the ability to plan, organize, and execute tasks. When we are stressed, we may have difficulty focusing, making decisions, and problem-solving. This can have negative effects on our work and personal life and may lead to feelings of frustration and overwhelm.

Additionally, stress can contribute to mental health problems such as anxiety and depression. These conditions can have further negative effects on brain health and cognitive function, leading to a vicious cycle of stress, poor mental health, and cognitive decline.

When I was in my early 20s right before cancer I was the most stressed I had ever been. My mind felt like mush most of the time, I was on edge and agitated often, and my gut-brain axis was completely disrupted.

Because emotionally I wasn't able to handle stress it had to go somewhere. It leaked out into my body in the form of constant stress hormones and disruptions to the brain like what you just read.

This all led me to be in a very unhealthy state psychologically, which led to me being unhealthy physically.

This is why this section is dedicated to brain hacks that will reduce stress.

Breathwork

There are a few different kinds of stress. There's the stress that's low-level and chronic. And there's the stress that's high-intensity and anxiety-inducing.

This section is more for handling the second when you're in a state of high stress and need some immediate relief.

#23: Box Breathing

Box breathing is a technique that involves slow, deep breathing to help reduce stress and promote relaxation. Here are the steps to follow for box breathing:

1. Find a quiet and comfortable place to sit or lie down.
2. Close your eyes and take a few deep breaths to relax your body and focus your mind.
3. Breathe in slowly and deeply through your nose for a count of four.
4. Hold your breath for a count of four.

5. Exhale slowly and completely through your mouth for a count of four.
6. Hold your breath again for a count of four before inhaling again.
7. Repeat the process for several minutes, or as long as you need to feel relaxed and calm.

The "box" in box breathing refers to the idea that each phase of the breathing cycle should be the same length, forming a square or box shape. By focusing on your breath and slowing it down, you can help to calm your nervous system and reduce feelings of stress and anxiety.

#24: Andrew Huberman's Two-Inhale Breathwork

Andrew Huberman, a neuroscientist and professor at Stanford University, has developed a breathing technique for quick stress reduction. Here's how it works:

1. Sit comfortably in a quiet place
2. Inhale deeply through your nose
3. Then at the top of the inhale do another big, quick, inhale
4. Exhale slowly and completely through your mouth for a count of 6 to 8 seconds.
5. Repeat the process for several cycles, 3 to 4 times, or as long as you need to feel relaxed and calm.

The idea behind the two inhale breaths is to increase the amount of oxygen in your body and activate your parasympathetic nervous system, which helps to promote relaxation and reduce stress. The longer exhale also helps to slow down your heart rate and promote relaxation.

#25: Get moving

Sometimes when you're feeling maxed out and stressed the best thing to do is to move your body. I don't mean do a 30-minute HIIT session but instead go walk around the block, if it's a safe neighborhood, for 5 to 10 minutes.

If I get an intense email from a client or partner that puts me in that immediate stress state I'll typically do a few rounds of breathwork then go walking. It always helps me get rid of that acute fearful stressed state.

When you're body is in the flight or fight stage, the act of walking and moving forward can work with its natural programming. You see, the body wants to move when it's in that state, by you sitting at your desk or on the couch you keep your body from eradicating the stress chemicals flooding your body.

By walking, you move in a forward motion and allow the body to shuttle the hormones and other molecules around. Allowing them to go through their natural

Also, walking can be a meditative experience, allowing you to focus on the present moment, your breathing, and your surroundings. This kind of mindfulness can help you take a break from stressors, clear your mind, and gain a new perspective on situations.

It can also serve as a healthy distraction from stressors, allowing you to take a break from daily demands and focus on something else. This can help you recharge and return to your tasks with a refreshed mindset.

Walking outdoors exposes you to natural environments unless you're in a city with high-rises all around you, which can have a calming effect. Research has shown that spending time in nature can reduce stress, improve mood, and enhance cognitive function.

#26: Sauna secrets: unwinding through heat

Breathwork and walking around the block are great ways to deal with immediate stress.

But when we have more chronic stress that's where saunas can help out. We will delve into the fascinating world of saunas and explore how they can be used to manage stress and promote relaxation.

The Science Behind Sauna and Stress Relief
Saunas work their magic by exposing the body to high temperatures, usually between 150°F and 200°F (65°C and 93°C). This heat stimulates the production of endorphins, which are natural pain-relieving chemicals that enhance feelings of well-being.

The heat prompts the body to release stress-related hormones, such as cortisol and encourages deep relaxation through the promotion of alpha brainwave activity. Regular sauna use can help to reduce stress levels, boost mood, and improve overall mental health.

The benefits of sauna use go beyond the physical, as it also serves as a mental escape. The warm, dimly lit environment of a sauna encourages introspection and reflection, helping to clear the mind and alleviate stress. As you sit in the soothing heat, you can focus on your breathing and practice mindfulness, which has been shown to reduce anxiety and improve mental well-being.

To maximize the stress-reducing effects of sauna use, it is essential to establish a consistent routine. Consider the following rituals to enhance your experience:

- Practice deep breathing: Focus on your breath as you inhale deeply through your nose and exhale slowly through your mouth. This practice can help to calm the mind and reduce stress.
- Stretch: Gentle stretching before or after your sauna session can help to release muscle tension and improve relaxation.

The Health Benefits of Sauna Bathing: Cardiovascular and All-Cause Mortality

In a 2015 study, Laukkanen et al. examined the sauna bathing habits of 2,315 Finnish men aged 42 to 60 years, who were participants in the Finnish Kuopio Ischemic Heart Disease Risk Factor Study from 1984 to 1989.

These men were followed for more than two decades to investigate the relationship between sauna bathing and fatal cardiovascular and all-cause mortality events. The study found that the more frequently the men used a sauna, the lower their risk of dying from cardiovascular disease, coronary artery disease, and all-cause mortality.

These findings suggest that regular sauna bathing may have potential health benefits, particularly in terms of cardiovascular health.

Integrating Sauna Sessions into Your Stress Management Plan

To reap the full benefits of sauna use for stress management, consistency is key. Aim for two to three sauna sessions per week, each lasting approximately 15-20 minutes. It's essential to listen to your body and adjust the frequency and duration of sessions according to your personal comfort level.

I've done the sauna many of times but I don't always have access to one. Purchasing can range in the thousands of dollars. If you find you thoroughly enjoy the sauna you can typically find them in big box gyms, specific "biohacking" studios, and bath houses you can get memberships at.

Incorporating sauna sessions into your overall stress management plan can make a significant difference in your mental and emotional well-being. As you embrace the warmth and serenity of the sauna, you'll find yourself feeling more relaxed, focused, and rejuvenated.

Meditation

Coming from stress management we now head into meditation. Meditation is good for creating a clearer mind, stronger presence and the ability to focus for longer periods of time.

In today's fast-paced world, it's increasingly challenging to maintain a clear mind, a strong presence, and the ability to focus for long periods of time. However, these qualities are essential for achieving success, fostering creativity, and maintaining mental well-being.

In this chapter, we will explore various meditation strategies and techniques to help you cultivate these traits, enabling you to unlock your full potential and navigate the complexities of modern life.

#27: Mindfulness meditation

The first profound shift in my mental state due to meditation occurred at a self-improvement workshop in California. It was a huge event with thousands in attendance. The facilitator led a group meditation session for everyone present. The experience was deeply impactful and has stayed with me ever since.

Practicing what I learned there reminded me of the importance of being mindful of my thoughts and acting as an observer within my own mind. This guidance set me on a journey towards regaining mastery over my thoughts and emotions.

There's a quote I love, "The mind is a horrible master but a great slave." The exact origin of this quote is uncertain. Regardless of its source, the quote emphasizes the importance of cultivating a healthy relationship with the mind and using it as a tool for getting what we truly desire, living a peaceful and happy life rather than allowing it to control and dominate our lives.

Mindfulness meditation history

Mindfulness meditation is a powerful practice that has been embraced by people across the globe for thousands of years. By helping individuals develop greater self-awareness, mental clarity, and emotional balance, mindfulness meditation can transform lives and foster inner peace.

The practice of mindfulness meditation can be traced back to ancient Eastern traditions, particularly Buddhism and Hinduism. These traditions emphasize the importance of cultivating present-moment awareness and developing a deep understanding of the nature of the mind and reality. Mindfulness meditation was developed as a means of achieving these goals.

Buddhism, which originated in ancient India over 2,500 years ago, is perhaps the most well-known tradition associated with mindfulness meditation. The Buddha taught that all suffering arises from the mind and that by developing a deep understanding of the mind, we can alleviate our own suffering and that of others. Mindfulness meditation was one of the key practices taught by the Buddha, and it continues to be an essential component of Buddhist practice today.

Over the past few decades, mindfulness meditation has gained widespread popularity in the Western world, largely due to the efforts of pioneers such as Jon Kabat-Zinn and Thich Nhat Hanh. Kabat-Zinn developed the Mindfulness-Based Stress Reduction (MBSR) program and is known as the father of modern mindfulness meditation. Hanh, a Vietnamese Zen master, has written extensively about the practice of mindfulness and its potential to transform individuals and society.

Today, mindfulness meditation is widely practiced by people of all backgrounds and belief systems. It has been embraced by a variety of secular institutions, including schools, hospitals, and businesses, as a means of promoting well-being and enhancing performance. The popularity of mindfulness meditation continues to grow as more people discover its profound benefits for mental, emotional, and physical health.

Basic Mindfulness Meditation Techniques

Mindfulness meditation involves focusing your attention on the present moment with an attitude of openness and non-judgment. There are several different techniques you can use to develop mindfulness, and each approach has its unique benefits. In this section, we will explore some of the most common mindfulness meditation techniques.

Breath Awareness: This technique involves focusing your attention on the sensation of your breath as it moves in and out of your body. You can choose to focus on the movement of your belly or the sensation of air moving in and out of your nostrils. As you focus on your breath, you may notice that your mind starts to wander. When this happens, simply notice the distraction and gently redirect your attention back to your breath.

Body Scan: In this technique, you bring your attention to different parts of your body, starting at the top of your head and working your way down to your toes. As you focus on each body part, you can observe any sensations, tension, or discomfort without judgment. This technique can help you become more aware of your physical sensations and develop a deeper connection with your body.

Sound Meditation: This technique involves focusing your attention on sounds around you, such as the sound of birds singing, traffic passing by, or people talking. As you focus on the sounds, try to observe them without judgment or analysis, simply noticing them as they arise and pass away.

Putting It Into Practice: 10 minutes
1. Find a quiet space and sit comfortably.
2. Take a few deep breaths, using the breathwork techniques previously mentioned and bringing your awareness to your breath
3. For the next few minutes, bring your awareness to your body and begin the body scan
4. Finally, watch the thoughts that come up for you and just observe them, with no judgment, remaining as present in the moment as possible

For biohacking tech, we'll be reviewing a headset that will give real-time feedback on your brain activity through Electroencephalography (EEG).

Ice Ice Baby

#28 Cold Therapy

Cold therapy involves exposing the body to cold temperatures, in the form of cold water, cryotherapy, and even cold showers (if lacking access to cold water or cryotherapy), for therapeutic purposes. While cold therapy is commonly used for reducing inflammation, improving athletic performance, and enhancing recovery, recent research suggests that it may also have cognitive benefits for the brain.

Often times when people hear of cold therapy they get intimidated or scared by it because the temperatures can be so extreme; understandably.

While it does initially suck when you're first in it, you get more used to it. Over time it also helps build your discipline because you're moving towards what you feel resistant to and doing it anyway. It also builds more confidence because doing the scary thing eradicates fear over time - the fear gets smaller as the person gets bigger (spiritually and emotionally).

David Goggins on a podcast with Joe Rogan said, "Being in cold water makes you question everything...many dreams die while suffering."

He was saying how bad the cold water can suck. But on the other side of suck, you become stronger.

Joe Rogan posted a video of himself getting into a cold tub with a big chunk of ice at the top. As he pulled away the chunk of ice and lowered himself into the cold tub he went on to explain the benefits of why he likes embracing the cold suck when he said, "the benefits for resilience, the benefits for my mind and for inflammation for my body. My body feels so good. All my soreness that was part of ordinary life, a massive amount of that has been dissipated but I haven't stopped working out just as hard."

Joe's not the only one to praise the benefits of cold.

Andrew Huberman, Wim Hof, Ross Edgley, Ben Greenfield, Tony Robbins, Tim Ferriss, Dr. Rhonda Patrick, Peter Attia, Aubrey Marcus, Lewis Howes, Mark Sisson and many more have all said how great cold is for our health, longevity and mood.

Cold therapy has been suggested to benefit the brain by increasing the production of neurotransmitters, specifically norepinephrine and dopamine. These neurotransmitters play crucial roles in regulating mood, motivation, and attention, and their levels can be positively influenced by cold therapy.

Norepinephrine, also known as noradrenaline, is a neurotransmitter that functions as both a hormone and a chemical messenger in the brain. It plays a vital role in the body's stress response, alertness, and focus. Research suggests that exposure to cold temperatures can stimulate the release of norepinephrine, leading to increased alertness and enhanced cognitive function. The activation of the sympathetic nervous system, which occurs during cold exposure, triggers the release of norepinephrine in the brain, resulting in heightened mental clarity and attention.

Dopamine, often referred to as the "reward neurotransmitter," is associated with pleasure, motivation, and reinforcement. It is involved in the brain's reward system and helps regulate mood, motivation, and movement. Studies have shown that cold therapy can increase dopamine production in the brain, leading to potential mood-boosting effects. One study, specifically investigating the effects of whole-body cryotherapy, found that participants experienced increased blood levels of norepinephrine and dopamine after the sessions. This suggests that exposure to cold temperatures can potentially enhance mood and motivation by promoting the release of dopamine.

The precise mechanisms through which cold therapy influences neurotransmitter production are not yet fully understood. However, the release of norepinephrine and dopamine in response to cold exposure is believed to be part of the body's physiological adaptation to cold stress. Cold temperatures activate the sympathetic nervous system and trigger the release of stress hormones like norepinephrine, which in turn affects dopamine levels. These neurotransmitters, once released, can have widespread effects on various brain functions, contributing to improved mood, increased motivation, and enhanced attention.

Another way that cold therapy may benefit the brain is by improving blood flow and oxygenation. When the body is exposed to cold temperatures, blood vessels constrict, reducing blood flow to the affected area. However, when the body is rewarmed, blood vessels dilate, increasing blood flow and oxygenation. This improved circulation can benefit the brain by providing it with more oxygen and nutrients, which are essential for cognitive function.

Cold therapy may benefit the brain by reducing stress and promoting relaxation. When the body is exposed to cold temperatures, it triggers the release of endorphins, which are natural painkillers and mood enhancers. These endorphins can help to reduce stress and promote relaxation, which can in turn benefit cognitive function and mental well-being.

Overall, while more research is needed to fully understand the cognitive benefits of cold therapy, there is evidence to suggest that it may be a promising tool for enhancing brain function and improving mental well-being. However, it is important to note that cold therapy should be used with caution, as exposure to extremely cold temperatures can be dangerous if not done properly. It is recommended to consult with a healthcare professional before trying cold therapy, especially if you have any underlying medical conditions.

Cryotherapy

The first one on the list is cryotherapy. And it's probably the best out of all of the cold therapies listed here it's also the most expensive and difficult to have access to.

Cryotherapy is a piece of equipment that encapsulates a person and immerses them in extremely cold temperatures (can be below 130 degrees Celsius) for 2 to 3 minutes at a time. There are also other devices that don't get as cold and keep people in for a few minutes longer.

It can either be a full unit, kind of the size of a big sauna, or a one-person cryotherapy device where the person's head sticks out the top. Either way, the benefits of it are becoming more known to us and cryotherapy is becoming more popular because of it.

They can be found at specialized wellness centers around the world. There are entire businesses that only have cryotherapy. And also biohacking-type studios that have a cryotherapy device as part of their suite of equipment.

Cryotherapy For Depression and Mood

In the study, "Efficacy of the Whole-Body Cryotherapy as Add-on Therapy to Pharmacological Treatment of Depression - A Randomized Controlled Trial," they looked at whether exposing people with depression to very cold temperatures, known as whole-body cryotherapy (WBC), could improve their mood and quality of life.

They compared a group of people who had 10 sessions of WBC (-110°C till -160°C) to another group who had 10 sessions of exposure to temperatures that were not as cold (-50°C).

The study found that the WBC group had a significant improvement in their depressive symptoms and quality of life compared to the other group. The study suggests that WBC can be a useful addition to traditional treatment for depression, but more research is needed to understand how it works.

Cold plunge tub

Cold plunge tubs, also known as cold plunge pools, are pools filled with cold water, typically maintained at temperatures between 50-55°F (10-13°C). These tubs are used for a form of hydrotherapy called cold water immersion. They can cost upwards of $10,000 to own one.

The history of cold plunge tubs can be traced back to various ancient civilizations that used cold water immersion as part of their bathing and wellness rituals.

Romans were known for their elaborate bathing rituals, which often included a series of hot, warm, and cold baths. The frigidarium was the cold bath area in Roman bathhouses, where bathers would plunge into cold water after experiencing the warmer pools. This practice was believed to promote circulation, rejuvenate the body, and improve overall health.

The Greek physician Hippocrates, often referred to as the "Father of Medicine," documented the use of cold water immersion as a therapeutic treatment for various ailments. Greeks also practiced hydrotherapy in their gymnasiums and palaestras, where cold baths were used alongside hot steam rooms and warm baths.

Japanese onsen, or natural hot spring baths, sometimes include cold plunge pools. These cold pools are used in conjunction with hot mineral baths to encourage circulation, relieve muscle aches, and promote relaxation.

Cold water immersion has long been a part of Nordic and Scandinavian bathing traditions. Sauna users would often jump into a cold lake, river, or plunge pool after spending time in the heat to invigorate the body and improve circulation.

Throughout history, cold plunge tubs and cold water immersion have been used for therapeutic purposes, with people from various cultures recognizing their potential health benefits.

In modern times, cold plunge tubs have become popular in spas, wellness centers, and athletic training facilities, where they are often used alongside hot tubs, saunas, and steam rooms as part of a contrast therapy routine.

Ice bath

The traditional cold therapy used in so many Hollywood movies, sports centers and backyards is, of course, ice baths. It involves submerging the body, or specific body parts, in cold water filled with ice for a short period, usually ranging from 10 to 20 minutes. The water temperature in an ice bath typically ranges from 50-59°F (10-15°C).

This is one of the most economical ways to use cold therapy as it just requires a tub, most modern homes have that, and bags of ice tossed in the water.

Cold showers

If these other cold therapies are out of reach for you then cold showers may be your best option. And for most people cold showers are going to be the most easily accessible and cheapest form of cold therapy. Although they don't get in the super cold ranges of cryotherapy equipment, they do still provide the benefits of cold therapy.

Take Alex's story for example

Alex, a software engineer who worked long hours and often felt mentally fatigued and drained. He struggled with brain fog, lack of focus, and low energy levels, which made it difficult to stay productive and engaged in his work.

One day, Alex stumbled upon an article about cold therapy and its potential benefits for mental cognition, mood, and energy levels. Intrigued, he decided to give it a try and began incorporating cold showers into his daily routine.

At first, the cold showers were uncomfortable and even a little painful, but Alex persevered and continued to do them regularly. He gradually increased the length and intensity of the showers, and over time, he began to notice a significant improvement in his mental clarity and energy levels.

He found that the cold therapy helped to wake him up and increase his alertness, making it easier to focus on his work and stay engaged throughout the day. He also noticed that his mood had improved, and he felt more positive and motivated.

As he continued to use cold therapy, Alex became a firm believer in its benefits for mental cognition, mood, and energy levels. He even started to experiment with other forms of cold therapy, such as ice baths and cryotherapy, and found that they too helped to boost his cognitive function and energy levels.

Overall, cold therapy became an important part of Alex's daily routine, helping him to overcome his mental fatigue and achieve greater success in his work and personal life.

Cold showers have gained attention for their potential health benefits, and several studies have been conducted to investigate these claims. While the research on cold showers is still somewhat limited, some studies have suggested potential benefits, such as improved circulation, increased alertness, and strengthened immune response. Here are a few examples:

Increased alertness:
Cold showers can stimulate the body's sympathetic nervous system, leading to a release of hormones like adrenaline and noradrenaline, which can increase alertness and wakefulness. A 2007 study published in Medical Hypotheses found that cold showers might help alleviate depressive symptoms by activating the sympathetic nervous system and increasing the release of these hormones.

Strengthened immune response:
A 2016 study published in PLOS ONE investigated the effects of a routine involving cold showers on sickness absence from work. Participants who took a cold shower daily reported a 29% reduction in sickness absence compared to the control group. The showers they took were normal warm showers and at the end, they turned the cold water on for 30 to 90 seconds. The study suggested that cold showers might help strengthen the immune system and improve overall health.

Improved mood and stress management:
Cold showers have been suggested to help with mood improvement and stress management by stimulating the release of endorphins, the body's natural pain-relieving and mood-enhancing hormones. A 2008 study published in Medical Hypotheses found that cold water exposure could potentially be used as a treatment for depression due to its ability to increase endorphin levels.

Keeping It In Mind

In the Trolls section in part one I talked about the Mentropy Toll; mental entropy. How the mind can move to chaotic, anxious and stressful thinking at times in our life. Like every other human, I've experienced significant amounts of this.

I didn't initially want to include a section like this in this book about biohacks because this isn't really a biohack. It's not a cool device, or fun supplement, or way of shocking the nervous system like 37 degree water does.

But I wanted to include this because it's an incredibly important section. It's how we can combat the Mentropy Troll time periods of our life. And it's been a big driving factor in my life.

When I was a teenager, life was confusing. I didn't understand people. I didn't like school, and it felt like a drag which reflected in my average"C" grades, and my future was a hazy, undefined path. It often felt like life was driving me, rather than the other way around.

Then at 17 years old I came across the book The Power of Now. I mentioned it earlier in this book but it really opened my thought process to an expanded way of experiencing life.

I went from being one thing that had no control to now separating my mind from my spirit, or soul, and other elements of self. I realized that I wasn't bound to the whims of my inner voice. For the first time, I was in the driver's seat. Of course, there were times the voice tried to take control, but I now had the reins. For at least a short while.

This section is going briefly into depth of how I learned to get power over my behavior, thoughts and actions. And how I failed miserably at it. And in the long run, how I learned to dominate my thoughts, actions, and overall behavior.

#29 The Pursuit of Inner Peace

One Wednesday evening in 2008, under the soft glow of my dorm room's wooden lampshade, I turned the final pages of "The Power of Now." I was deeply moved, experiencing an entirely new perspective – I was observing my thoughts rather than being absorbed in them.

The main idea of the book was the mantra, "Live in the present moment." It was a radical idea for me, with a mind that felt more like a hyperactive whirlwind. Retrospectively, the ADHD label explained a lot. My thoughts often felt like an untamed horse that's been locked away for too long, suddenly set free.

Embracing the present was a challenge. Not because I couldn't focus for brief moments, but when I truly immersed myself in the 'now,' the world seemed a tad too intense.

The very next day, during my shift at Moe's Southwest Grille, ("welcome to Moe's!") I tried implementing this newfound wisdom. Standing there, leaning on the cool metal of the cook table, I tried to shut off my thoughts, simply observing. But when a customer approached, expecting the usual jovial banter, I found myself at a loss. My typical humor had vanished, and I felt oddly incomplete in that moment.

Jumping to San Francisco, 2014. By now you're aware that my professional environment at that time wasn't the healthiest for me, mentally or physically. It wasn't a reflection on the company or my colleagues; I was just navigating a turbulent phase of my life.

One day, already irritated by a mistake I'd made and battling repetitive gut pain, I approached a coworker and inquired, "Where are the last two orders? The boss needs them!"

Unexpectedly, she erupted in anger — unusual for someone typically so composed. The specifics of the exchange escape me now, but the aftermath was clear. I angrily shuffled back to my desk, immobilized.

That brief, tumultuous encounter replayed in my mind on a continuous loop for hours. It became my torturous soundtrack, reinforcing my ongoing pattern of rumination that had intensified over the past eight months.

After enduring this mental carousel for a while, I decided to clear the air. We stepped outside and talked it out, both expressing regret for our reactions. Despite our resolution, the physical stress of the confrontation, manifesting in eye strain and stomach discomfort, continued to plague me. My mind then shifted gears, dredging up a disagreement from the previous week. I was trapped in the past, not savoring the gift of the present.

Fast forward to today: things are vastly different. While I'm no sage or spiritual guru, I've honed a deeper sense of inner peace. For the most part, I'm rooted in the here and now. Even when my mind races, I've learned to rein it in. I can quickly snap back to the present and intercept negative spirals before they gain traction.

Over time, I've recognized the mind's sneaky tactics to dominate us, the "Observers". Whether it's stoking fear, magnifying mishaps, or enticing us with delusions of grandeur, the mind knows no bounds.

Breaking free from this endless cycle demands presence. Force your brain to activate and be sharp and observe everything around you. Engage fully with your surroundings. Connect genuinely in conversations. Ground yourself, whether you're in a meeting or simply contemplating in solitude. Embrace the tranquility within; that's my approach, at least.

Hopefully, my journey offers some solace or guidance. Always remember, while you may not have control over every fleeting thought, you decide which ones to dwell on. Think of thoughts as transient headlines scrolling on a news ticker; let them come and go, anchoring yourself in the present.

Electrolytes

#30 Electrolytes

As mentioned in the Water Troll chapter, a lack of electrolytes is becoming a bigger problem for us. If you recall, neurons, the primary cells of the nervous system, communicate through electrical impulses. These impulses, or action potentials, require a delicate dance of electrolytes, particularly sodium and potassium, moving in and out of the neuron.

When we think, move, feel, or remember, we do so because countless neurons are transmitting signals. An imbalance in electrolytes, especially sodium and potassium, can impair this delicate process. Brain fog can be a direct outcome of this impairment. Proper electrolyte balance ensures smooth neural communication, making it pivotal for clear thinking and optimal cognitive function.

Also, electrolytes, especially sodium and potassium, help balance the body's fluids. They prevent both dehydration and overhydration, ensuring that the brain and other organs have the right fluid balance to function. Regularly consuming water and maintaining electrolyte balance is crucial for cognitive health and preventing brain fog associated with dehydration.

You want to look for a low-calorie electrolyte combo so that you're not loading up with sugar and if you do this while fasting you won't break the fast. You can find numerous powder options of these on Amazon or other retailers online.

I'll typically put a serving in my water in the morning while fasting. This helps keep my hunger levels low and attention up. Speaking of fasting.

No Food

#31 Intermittent Fasting

For centuries, fasting has been a ritual and therapeutic practice across various cultures and religions. While many engage in fasting for spiritual reasons, the physiological and cognitive benefits are becoming increasingly recognized in the scientific community. It's one of my go-to's daily for improved energy and presence. This chapter delves deep into how fasting can enhance attention, energy, and focus, exploring the mechanisms that underpin these improvements.

Intermittent fasting is when you go without food for a certain amount of time. A common time is 16:8. What this means is that you'll go 16 hours without eating and then have an 8-hour eating window. That could mean stopping eating at 8 p.m. and not eating again until 12 p.m. the next day. There are other means of fasting as well, such as 18:6, 20:4, 24-hour fasts, 48-hour fasts and so on.

When one fasts, the body undergoes a plethora of neurochemical changes. For starters, fasting increases the production of norepinephrine, a neurotransmitter involved in alertness and attention. Higher norepinephrine levels are thought to be the body's natural mechanism to increase alertness during times when food is scarce and hunting (or foraging) requires a sharper mind. Yes, these are part of the stress response at times so if you're in chronic stress and are finding yourself unable to keep stress levels low you may want to delay fasting until you balance out your recovery a bit more.

As previously mentioned, BDNF is a protein that plays a crucial role in neuroplasticity, neuronal growth, and overall brain health. Fasting has been shown to elevate BDNF levels. Increased BDNF not only supports neuronal health but also improves cognitive functions, especially memory and learning. With improved learning comes better focus, as a brain with optimized neural connections processes information more efficiently.

After fasting for about 12 to 16 hours, the body starts producing ketones. These molecules, derived from fat stores, are an alternative energy source for the brain. Compared to glucose, some believe ketones are considered a more efficient and stable energy source. This metabolic switch to using ketones is associated with enhanced cognitive clarity, energy, and focus.

Mitochondria, often dubbed the powerhouses of the cell, are where the cell's energy is produced. Fasting improves mitochondrial efficiency and biogenesis (production of new mitochondria). With more efficient energy production, neuronal cells function optimally, leading to improved attention and focus.

Whereas mitochondria handle the production side of things, autophagy is all about maintenance. Think of autophagy as the cell's recycling and waste management system. Old, malfunctioning, or damaged cellular components are enclosed in vesicles, and broken down, and the resulting materials are repurposed or expelled.

Fasting acts as a potent trigger for autophagy. In the absence of external nutrients, the cell initiates this 'clean-up' mode more aggressively. The brain, being a highly metabolically active organ, benefits immensely from this. Over time, due to oxidative stress and other factors, cellular components can become damaged. In neurons, this could impair signal transmission or other vital functions. Autophagy ensures these faulty parts are removed, maintaining the cell's efficiency.

Once the old components are cleared out, cells can synthesize new, functional ones. This renewal process is especially crucial for neurons, as they need to maintain optimal functionality for the brain to work well. Autophagy also plays a protective role. Getting rid of potentially toxic cellular waste prevents accumulation that could lead to neuronal damage or death.

In essence, while fasting, autophagy ensures neurons remain 'clean,' efficient, and functional. This directly contributes to cognitive improvements, notably in attention and focus.

Chronic inflammation is increasingly recognized as a culprit behind many health issues, from cardiovascular diseases to cognitive decline. At the cellular level, inflammation is essentially a defense mechanism, a response to injury or infection. However, when this response becomes chronic, it can wreak havoc, especially in the brain.

During fasting, the body goes into a state of conservation and repair. This process inadvertently reduces the overall inflammatory state of the body. Specifically, fasting decreases the production of pro-inflammatory cytokines, which are signaling proteins that promote inflammation.

Inflammation can be particularly detrimental to the brain. Inflammatory molecules can affect the integrity and function of neurons, which are pivotal for cognitive processes like attention and focus. By mitigating inflammation, fasting helps preserve neuronal health. A brain unburdened by inflammation operates more efficiently. It can process information better, maintain attention for extended periods, and mobilize energy optimally. The reduction in inflammation thus translates into palpable cognitive benefits.

Fasting is more than a dietary restriction. It's a physiological reset button, activating pathways and processes that rejuvenate the brain and enhance its function. While fasting isn't a one-size-fits-all remedy, understanding its potential can pave the way for individualized approaches to harness its cognitive benefits. Whether for spiritual, health, or cognitive reasons, incorporating mindful fasting practices could be a step toward a more attentive, energetic, and focused self.

Nootropics

Some say the term "nootropic" was first coined in the 1970s by the Romanian chemist Corneliu E. Giurgea, who defined it as a substance that enhances learning and memory and protects the brain from damage, without causing significant side effects.

Yet others say nootropics are derived from the Greek words "noos" which means "mind" and "tropos," which translates to "bend." They're quite mind-bending, Neo, there is no spoon.

Wherever they come from, nootropics are known as cognitive enhancers and are substances that are used to improve cognitive function, concentration, memory, and mental clarity, without causing significant side effects.

How Do Nootropics Work

There are four main ways nootropics work to enhance cognitive performance, stimulate new nerve growth or improve memory.

1. Modulation of Neurotransmitters

Many nootropics work by modulating neurotransmitter systems in the brain. Neurotransmitters are chemicals that transmit signals between neurons, and different neurotransmitters are involved in various cognitive functions.

For example, acetylcholine is important for memory and attention, while dopamine is involved in motivation and reward. By enhancing or inhibiting the activity of certain neurotransmitters, nootropics can affect cognitive processes such as memory, attention, and mood.

Think about it this way. You know when driving you have green lights and red lights. Imagine you're coming home through a road that has light after light after light. Nootropics that enhance acetylcholine are like having a bunch of green lights. Then other nootropics that inhibit neurotransmitters are like throwing yellow and red lights in there.

With a bunch of green lights, the brain will be lit up and firing on all cylinders.

2. Antioxidants - Be Gone Radicals!
Some nootropics act as antioxidants, reducing oxidative stress in the brain. Oxidative stress is a process that can damage cells and contribute to neurodegenerative diseases, and some nootropics have been shown to protect against this damage.

3. Blood Flow Is King
Some nootropics increase blood flow and oxygen delivery to the brain, which can enhance brain function. For example, compounds such as vinpocetine and ginkgo biloba have been shown to increase blood flow to the brain and improve cognitive performance.

4. I Gotta Survive - The Last Of Us Up In Here
Some nootropics promote the growth and survival of neurons in the brain. For example, compounds such as brain-derived neurotrophic factor (BDNF) and nerve growth factor (NGF) are important for the growth and maintenance of neurons, and some nootropics have been shown to increase the levels of these compounds in the brain.

A More Subtle Approach

Nootropics are all the buzz happening at the moment. Most nootropic supplements don't hit you like a ton of bricks but instead, slowly guide you to increased concentration and brain power.

While certain drugs like central nervous system (CNS) stimulants - Ritalin or Adderall, for instance - can indeed enhance brain function, their usage in the biohacking context is typically avoided. These substances have the potential to trigger adverse side effects such as anxiety, irritability, raising blood pressure and insomnia - outcomes that don't align with the concept of nootropics as defined by the renowned chemist Corneliu E. Giurgea.

Giurgea, who coined the term "nootropics", stated that such substances must have minimal or no side effects, thereby fostering cognitive improvements without negatively affecting the user's health. In this light, the widespread usage of CNS stimulants doesn't fit into the nootropic discussion, given the considerable side effects they often produce.

An important aspect to consider is the physiological effect of these stimulants. They trigger the body's "fight or flight" response, also known as the sympathetic state. This hyperactive state is opposed to the parasympathetic state, which promotes rest, relaxation, and recovery. When the body is constantly in a sympathetic state, there is insufficient time for rest and recuperation, which could lead to health complications such as high blood pressure.

That said, it's crucial to note that this book doesn't aim to demonize CNS stimulants - they have their place in specific scenarios and can be useful under the right circumstances. However, the current societal use of these substances often strays from their original intent. They are frequently overprescribed and used for prolonged periods, far beyond the duration they were initially intended for. This misuse and overuse present significant health concerns and are the key reasons why they are generally excluded from the nootropic category in biohacking.

But slow down there Magneto, you have to be sure you're taking the right kind for your goal.

Some are meant to help slow you down and reduce anxiety, such as Gaba. While others are aimed at full focus mode, such as Alpha GPC.

Below are the nootropics I've personally found to be useful. This is of course not an exhaustive list and please check with your healthcare professional before doing any of these if you have medical conditions. Supplements may interact with medications so please speak to your doctor first.

Nine Supplements For Energy, Focus and Cognitive Enhancement

Before you rush off to consume all these supplements simultaneously in hopes of achieving ultra-concentration, it's crucial to realize that some of these may interact. They may have similar actions within the body, meaning they can influence the same processes but in varied ways.

So, taking them all together won't necessarily translate to a 900% increase in brain power. The supplements I've mentioned fall under different categories of nootropics. They have been shown by research, and my own personal experience aligns, to enhance various brain functions. However, their effects need to be considered individually, rather than expecting a cumulative or multiplicative effect. And if you're taking medication or have other health issues definitely speak to your doctor first as they may have some interactions.

#32: Alpha-GPC

Alpha-GPC is a naturally occurring compound found in small amounts in various foods, such as eggs, milk, soy, and some meats. It can also be synthesized and taken as a dietary supplement. Alpha-GPC is a precursor to the neurotransmitter acetylcholine, which plays a crucial role in various cognitive processes, including learning, memory, and attention.

Some studies suggest that Alpha-GPC may improve cognitive function in healthy individuals. This could include enhanced memory, learning, attention, and mental clarity.

Research has shown that Alpha-GPC may be beneficial for individuals experiencing age-related cognitive decline or mild cognitive impairment. A review of clinical trials published in 2013 found that Alpha-GPC supplementation improved cognitive function in older adults with mild to moderate Alzheimer's disease or other forms of dementia. It is thought that the increase in acetylcholine production may contribute to these effects.

It also has been found to have neuroprotective properties, potentially helping to protect brain cells from damage caused by various factors, such as aging, injury, or oxidative stress. This may help maintain overall brain health and function.

This is my favorite nootropic. I've found it works the best for me personally. And at the end of going through the rest of these I'll share with you my nootropic stack right now. It's probably more simple than you'll expect.

#33: L-theanine

L-theanine is an amino acid that is found in tea and has been shown to promote relaxation and reduce anxiety. It may also enhance cognitive function and improve mood by increasing the production of neurotransmitters such as serotonin and dopamine.

Some research suggests that L-theanine may improve cognitive function and increase focus, especially when combined with caffeine. A study published in the journal Nutritional Neuroscience in 2008 found that the combination of L-theanine and caffeine improved cognitive performance and alertness in healthy participants. This may be due to the synergistic effects of L-theanine's relaxation properties and caffeine's stimulant effects.

It may help improve mood by increasing the production of neurotransmitters such as serotonin and dopamine, which play a crucial role in regulating mood, sleep, and overall well-being. While more research is needed to confirm these findings, some studies have shown promising results.

I like to put this in my morning water along with electrolytes while fasting. Then I put my cold coffee in another cup and drink it black. So I get my electrolytes with L-theanine in one cup and coffee in another. I tried putting L-theanine in my coffee but since I drink it cold it didn't blend in well together. It left me drinking chunks of power. But in the water, it seems to blend in better for some reason.

#34: Huperzine A

Huperzine A, is a naturally occurring alkaloid derived from the Chinese club moss plant (Huperzia serrata). Huperzine A has been traditionally used in Chinese medicine and has gained interest in recent years for its potential effects on memory and cognitive function.

Huperzine A has been shown to improve memory and cognitive function, primarily through its ability to inhibit the enzyme acetylcholinesterase. This enzyme is responsible for breaking down acetylcholine, a neurotransmitter that plays a crucial role in learning, memory, and other cognitive processes. By inhibiting acetylcholinesterase, Huperzine A helps increase acetylcholine levels in the brain, potentially enhancing cognitive performance.

Some studies have suggested that Huperzine A may have antidepressant-like effects, possibly by increasing levels of certain neurotransmitters, such as norepinephrine, dopamine, and serotonin.

#35: Bacopa monnieri

Bacopa monnieri, is an herb that has been traditionally used in Ayurvedic medicine for its potential cognitive benefits and mood-enhancing properties.

Bacopa has been shown to improve memory and cognitive function in both healthy individuals and those with cognitive impairments. It may work by enhancing the communication between nerve cells, promoting the growth of new neurons, and protecting against oxidative stress.

Bacopa monnieri has been studied for its potential anxiolytic (anxiety-reducing) and adaptogenic (stress-resistance) properties. It is believed to help balance stress hormones, such as cortisol and support the body's ability to cope with stress.

Bacopa monnieri may help improve mood by modulating the levels of certain neurotransmitters, such as serotonin, dopamine, and noradrenaline, which play a crucial role in regulating mood, sleep, and overall well-being.

#36: Cordyceps Sinensis

Cordyceps Sinensis is a species of fungus that has been used in traditional Chinese medicine for its various health benefits. It is believed to possess adaptogenic properties, which means it may help the body adapt to various stressors, maintain homeostasis, and support overall vitality. This can be particularly helpful in situations of physical or mental stress, fatigue, or illness.

As a cognitive enhancer, Cordyceps Sinensis is thought to improve brain function, increase energy levels, and enhance mental clarity. It may also boost the immune system and promote overall wellness.

Some research suggests that Cordyceps sinensis may increase energy levels and improve athletic performance by enhancing the body's ability to utilize oxygen and produce energy (ATP) more efficiently.

It also contains compounds with antioxidant properties, which can help protect cells from damage caused by free radicals and oxidative stress. This may contribute to its potential benefits for brain health, immune function, and overall wellness.

#37: Reishi

Reishi, also known as Ganoderma lucidum, is a medicinal mushroom that has been used in traditional Chinese medicine for its immune-boosting and stress-relieving properties.

It's also been studied for its potential effects on mental clarity, focus, and anxiety reduction. While more research is needed to confirm these findings, some studies suggest that Reishi may improve cognitive function through its antioxidant and anti-inflammatory properties, which can help protect brain cells from damage and maintain overall brain health.

Reishi is considered an adaptogen, which means it may help the body adapt to various stressors and maintain homeostasis. It is believed to help balance stress hormones and support the body's ability to cope with stress, which can have a positive impact on mood and overall well-being.

It contains compounds with antioxidant and anti-inflammatory properties, which can help protect cells from damage caused by free radicals and oxidative stress. This may contribute to its potential benefits for brain health, immune function, and overall wellness.

#38: Lion's Mane

Lion's Mane is probably the most popular nootropic and mushroom for focus on the market today. You'll see Lion's mane in everything from coffee, energy drinks, chocolate, protein bars and more. It's definitely one of my favorites.

Lion's Mane (Hericium erinaceus) is a type of medicinal mushroom known for its distinctive appearance resembling a lion's mane. It has a long history of use in traditional Chinese medicine and has gained popularity in recent years for its potential cognitive benefits as a nootropic.

As a nootropic, Lion's Mane is believed to enhance cognitive function, improve memory, and support overall brain health. It contains bioactive compounds, including hericenones and erinacines, which are thought to contribute to its neurological effects.

One of the key ways Lion's Mane may benefit cognitive function is by promoting the production of nerve growth factor (NGF). NGF is a protein that plays a crucial role in the growth, maintenance, and survival of nerve cells. By stimulating NGF synthesis, Lion's Mane may support the regeneration and protection of brain cells, potentially improving memory, focus, and overall cognitive performance.

Studies have shown promising results regarding the cognitive effects of Lion's Mane. For example, a study published in the Journal of Agricultural and Food Chemistry found that Lion's Mane extract improved spatial recognition memory in mice. Another study published in the International Journal of Medicinal Mushrooms reported positive effects on cognitive function and quality of life in elderly individuals with mild cognitive impairment after daily consumption of Lion's Mane extract for several months.

Additionally, Lion's Mane may have potential neuroprotective properties. Research suggests that it may help reduce inflammation and oxidative stress in the brain, which are factors associated with age-related cognitive decline and neurodegenerative diseases like Alzheimer's and Parkinson's.

While Lion's Mane shows promise as a nootropic, it's important to note that further research is still needed to fully understand its mechanisms of action and therapeutic potential in humans. As with any supplement, it's advisable to consult with a healthcare professional before incorporating Lion's Mane or any other nootropic into your routine, especially if you have any underlying medical conditions or are taking medications.

In summary, Lion's Mane is a mushroom with potential cognitive benefits. It may support cognitive function, memory, and brain health through its ability to promote the production of nerve growth factor and its potential neuroprotective effects. However, more research is needed to fully understand its effects and determine optimal dosage and long-term safety.

#39: Ginkgo Biloba

Ginkgo Biloba is an herb that has been used for centuries to enhance memory and cognitive function. It contains powerful antioxidants called flavonoids and terpenoids, which protect brain cells from oxidative stress and inflammation. It's also known to improve blood flow to the brain, providing additional oxygen and nutrients that can help support healthy brain function. As a cognitive enhancer, Ginkgo Biloba is thought to improve memory, focus, and mental clarity, while also reducing mental fatigue.

It also contains powerful antioxidants, such as flavonoids and terpenoids, which can help protect brain cells from damage caused by free radicals and oxidative stress. This may contribute to its potential benefits for brain health and cognitive function.

It has been shown to have anti-inflammatory properties, which may help reduce inflammation in the brain and support overall cognitive health.

#40: Ashwagandha

Ashwagandha, also known as Withania somnifera, is an adaptogenic herb that has been used in Ayurvedic medicine to reduce stress, improve memory, and enhance cognitive function. Its active compounds, called withanolides, have been shown to support the production of neurotransmitters and help regulate stress hormones, such as cortisol, and support the body's ability to cope with stress. Additionally, Ashwagandha has been shown to promote neurogenesis, or the growth of new brain cells, which may contribute to its cognitive-enhancing effects.

It also has been shown to have anti-inflammatory effects, which may help reduce inflammation in the brain and support overall cognitive health.

My preference for ashwagandha is to use it to reduce stress. We reviewed the negative effects of stress earlier so I do everything I can to protect against it.

Of course, you don't have to take all of these at once. It's recommended to not do that. Instead, find ones that work for you personally and won't interact with any medications you're taking. Always speak to your doctor first if you're unsure.

Closing Nootropic Notes

Now that we've discussed several nootropics it's good to know that you can't just take all of them and have them synergistically add up on one another. Some may have competing mechanisms of action. Basically, they might fight for the same spots in your brain. It's nice to know what a working combo is.

I can't go into all the recipes of the mixes in this book but one go-to that's on the marketplace now, and my favorite, is alpha-gpc with bacopa and L-theanine. That three-ring combo seems to bring the brain up, while also leveling it out for all-day consistency.

Auditory Stimulation

One of my absolute go-to's is putting on headphones and getting in the zone while in a coffee shop. There's something about jamming out to the right kind of music and beats that'll get you in the zone like nothing else!

Auditory stimulation can be used to enhance focus by listening to certain kinds of music and binaural beats.

#41: Binaural Beats

Binaural beats are an auditory illusion created when two slightly different frequencies are played simultaneously to each ear, resulting in the perception of a third, "beat" frequency.

For example, if a 400 Hz tone is played in one ear and a 410 Hz tone is played in the other ear, the brain will perceive a beat frequency of 10 Hz, which is the difference between the two tones.

Binaural beats are believed to influence brainwave activity by encouraging the brain to synchronize its neural oscillations to the frequency of the perceived beat. Different binaural beat frequencies are associated with specific brainwave states:

Delta (1-4 Hz): Associated with deep sleep and relaxation
Theta (4-8 Hz): Linked to meditation, creativity, and REM sleep
Alpha (8-13 Hz): Associated with relaxation, light meditation, and increased focus

Beta (13-30 Hz): Linked to alertness, concentration, and cognitive tasks

Gamma (30-100 Hz): Associated with higher cognitive functioning and problem-solving

Many people use binaural beats as a tool to promote relaxation, meditation, focus, or sleep, depending on the frequency being used.

The easiest way to find binaural beats is by searching on YouTube for something like: "Binaural beats for focus" or "binaural beats for studying."

#42: Focus Music

In the realm of productivity hacks, one of the oft-recommended strategies is the use of music to amplify concentration. While it might seem counterintuitive to introduce an additional sensory input when attempting to concentrate, the trick lies in selecting the right kind of music. For many, including myself, the key is instrumental music.

Why Instrumental Over Lyrics?

Music with lyrics can be a double-edged sword. While they can emotionally resonate, making tasks feel less tedious, they can also serve as a source of distraction. It's not uncommon to find oneself humming along or getting lost in the narrative of the song, both of which divert focus from the task at hand.

Instrumental music, devoid of words, becomes less of a story and more of an ambiance. It creates a sonic backdrop against which our thoughts can freely flow, uninterrupted by lyrical interjections. The brain is not sidetracked by processing and interpreting words, allowing it to dedicate more resources to the task in front.

For me, I need to work to instrumental music only. This is because words from the songs can get caught in my head and distract me from my work. But if it's just background music then it can amplify my focus.

For example, I like listening to instrumental house or electronic music. I find that puts my mind in the best state for concentration.

I've also found that classical music can put me in a focus state as well. If I'm feeling overly stressed or anxious this is the one I tend to lean towards. Classical compositions often have intricate structures and progressions, and while they can be intense, they can also be incredibly calming. For moments when stress and anxiety threaten to impede productivity, classical tunes can serve as a balm, reducing the heart rate, calming the mind, and creating a serene environment conducive to deep focus.

Music, in its multifaceted forms, offers a diverse range of tools to aid focus. Whether it's the rhythmic drive of electronic beats or the tranquil harmonies of a classical symphony, the key is in finding what resonates with your cognitive rhythms. It's about trial and error, experimenting with different genres until you find that perfect auditory companion for your tasks. So, the next time you're gearing up for a productive session, consider tuning in and zoning out with your favorite instrumental track.

Headset Technology Devices

#43: BrainTap Headset

I was at a Biohacking conference in Orlando, Florida summer of 2023 and was feeling a bit stressed. I had traveled to get to this conference, had a difficult time getting through traffic and finally got my room key after a long wait. As I made my way through the conference I tried different biohacking technologies. A few of the ones I tried were good but I didn't really feel a big shift in state. Until I sat down at the BrainTap station.

BrainTap is a headset technology that blends light and sound frequencies to guide the brain into specific states of consciousness. By using visual and auditory stimuli, it's designed to synchronize and balance the brainwaves in both hemispheres of the brain. This state of synchronization, known as hemispheric synchronization or "whole brain" state, is believed to enhance focus, relaxation, sleep, and even learning.

After putting the headset on and giving it a try for 15 minutes I felt a huge shift in my nervous system. I knew I was in a sympathetic, stressed state before putting the headset on. Afterward, I felt my brain calm down and my body be more relaxed. I was able to think clearer, stay more present and converse with people more easily. After that experience, I immediately bought one and use it almost every day.

At the core of BrainTap's technology are binaural beats and pulsing lights. Binaural Beats are auditory processing artifacts that result from two slightly different frequencies being played in separate ears. The brain perceives a third tone as the mathematical difference between the two frequencies. For instance, if one ear hears a 300Hz tone and the other hears a 310Hz tone, the brain perceives a 10Hz binaural beat. These beats can guide the brain into states of relaxation, focus, meditation, or even deep sleep, depending on the frequency.

Coupled with the auditory stimulation, BrainTap uses visual stimulation through LED-equipped visors. The lights pulse at specific frequencies, aligning with the binaural beats to enhance the effect on the brain.

By guiding the brain into alpha and theta states, BrainTap claims to help users achieve deep relaxation. These states are associated with meditation and the early stages of sleep, respectively.

The technology can be used to prepare the mind for a restful night's sleep, potentially benefiting those with sleep disturbances.

Some users and practitioners claim that using BrainTap can help optimize the brain for learning and memory retention.

By helping balance brainwaves, BrainTap may aid in mood stabilization and the alleviation of symptoms related to anxiety and depression.

While many individuals swear by the benefits of BrainTap and similar technologies, it's essential to approach such devices with an open yet skeptical mind. The scientific community remains divided on the long-term effects and benefits of binaural beats and light therapy. Although there are studies indicating potential benefits, more research is needed to draw definitive conclusions.

BrainTap is a manifestation of our age-old quest to optimize the human experience, now armed with technology. It taps (pun intended) into the brain's inherent plasticity and adaptability, using auditory and visual stimuli to guide it into desired states. As with all such innovations, while early results and user testimonials may be promising, a blend of personal experience and evidence-based research will paint the clearest picture of its efficacy. If you're considering giving BrainTap a try, it might be worthwhile to start with an open mind, gauge personal results, and stay informed about emerging research on the topic.

#44: Muse Headset

Neurofeedback is a non-invasive technique that involves monitoring brainwave activity and providing real-time feedback to the user, allowing them to adjust their mental state accordingly. By observing their brainwave patterns and making conscious adjustments, users can learn to regulate their brain activity and achieve a more focused and attentive state.

The Muse headset, a brain-sensing headband, has emerged as a popular tool for individuals seeking to improve their meditation practice, mental clarity, and overall well-being.

The Muse headset works by utilizing electroencephalogram (EEG) technology to monitor brain activity in real-time. The device measures electrical signals produced by the brain and provides feedback on the user's mental state during meditation sessions. This real-time feedback helps users understand their current state of mind and make conscious adjustments to achieve deeper focus and relaxation.

Essentially, you wear the headset and meditate. Then there are bird noises that get louder as your brain activity increases. Indicating that you're getting away from the present through a stimulated brain. You hear the bird noises, it brings your awareness back to the present and then the birds quiet down again.

I always find I have a clearer head the next day after about 10 minutes the night before. It's not a big time investment and it'll help me get more present in every moment.

The Muse app tracks your meditation progress, providing insights into the duration, frequency, and quality of your sessions. This data helps users set goals, monitor improvements, and maintain motivation.

It also offers a variety of guided meditation sessions tailored to specific goals, such as stress reduction, improved focus, or better sleep. These sessions are led by experienced meditation instructors and can be customized to suit individual preferences.

Integration with Other Apps: Muse can be connected to various third-party apps, allowing users to explore different meditation techniques and practices while still benefiting from the real-time feedback provided by the headset.

Benefits of Using the Muse Headset

Improved Focus and Concentration
By providing real-time feedback during meditation sessions, the Muse headset helps users train their brains to maintain focus and avoid distractions more effectively.

Enhanced Meditation Practice
The guided meditation sessions and personalized tracking features of the Muse app allow users to deepen their meditation practice, resulting in increased mindfulness and mental clarity.

Stress Reduction
Regular meditation with the Muse headset can help users manage stress more effectively by promoting relaxation and mental resilience.

Better Sleep

The Muse app offers guided meditation sessions specifically designed to help users wind down and prepare for a restful night's sleep.

The Muse headset offers a unique and innovative approach to meditation, making it an attractive option for individuals seeking to improve their mental performance and overall well-being. By providing real-time feedback on brain activity, the device helps users train their minds to achieve better focus, concentration, and relaxation. If you're looking to enhance your meditation practice or explore new ways to unlock your mind's potential, the Muse headset might be the perfect tool to help you on your journey.

Conclusion

We examined what the Brain Boost formula is.

The Brain Boost Formula:
- Maximizing **Quality Input**
- Optimizing **Cellular Signaling**
- Beneficially adjusting our **Homeostasis**

Which is about putting quality ingredients into the body and signaling the body's cells to change in a way we want them to. Therefore creating a "boosted" state of being.

Next, we went over the 7 trolls of brain fog. These were: Tummy Troll (gut-brain axis), Water Troll, Endo Troll (endocrine system), Mentropy Troll (mental entropy), Cave Troll (physical inactivity), Oxy Troll (getting in enough oxygen), and lastly Pillow Troll (quality sleep).

You now have an extensive repertoire of 44 brain hacks that are designed to help you achieve increased mental clarity, energy, and focus. The journey toward a sharper, more efficient mind may seem daunting at first, but with consistent effort, patience, and the implementation of these strategies, you'll notice significant improvements in your cognitive performance.

It is important to remember that each individual is unique, and you may find that certain hacks work better for you than others. Feel free to experiment with the techniques provided, and be open to discovering new ways to optimize your brainpower. As you progress, keep track of the methods that work best for you and make adjustments as needed.

In today's rapidly changing world, keeping up-to-date with the latest advancements in neuroscience and cognitive psychology is crucial. As new research emerges, don't hesitate to incorporate these findings and methods into your brain-boosting routine. By staying informed and agile, you'll ensure that your cognitive enhancement strategies remain effective and cutting-edge.

As you continue to cultivate your mental prowess, you'll begin to notice a ripple effect in various areas of your life. Improved cognition can lead to better decision-making, heightened creativity, and increased productivity, all of which contribute to a more fulfilling existence. You may even discover that your relationships improve as your communication skills and empathy grow stronger.

In a world where knowledge is power, investing in your mental well-being is of utmost importance. By applying the principles outlined in The Brain Boost Formula, you're not only enhancing your cognitive performance but also paving the way for personal and professional success. The benefits of a sharper mind are manifold, and your commitment to self-improvement will yield rewards beyond your imagination.

Thank you for embarking on this transformative journey with us. As you continue to unlock the limitless potential of your brain, remember that persistence and determination are key. It may take time to see the full benefits of your efforts, but rest assured that your dedication will be well worth it in the end.

May your mind continue to expand, your energy levels soar, and your focus remain steadfast as you navigate the path to heightened mental clarity, energy, and focus. With The Brain Boost Formula as your guide, there's no doubt that a brighter, more empowered future awaits you.

Feel free to reach out me to at biohacktivity.com

References

1. Dresler M, Sandberg A, Bublitz C, Ohla K, Trenado C, Mroczko-Wąsowicz A, Kühn S, Repantis D. Hacking the Brain: Dimensions of Cognitive Enhancement. ACS Chem Neurosci. 2019 Mar 20;10(3):1137-1148. doi: 10.1021/acschemneuro.8b00571. Epub 2019 Jan 2. PMID: 30550256; PMCID: PMC6429408.
2. Colzato LS, Barone H, Sellaro R, Hommel B. More attentional focusing through binaural beats: evidence from the global-local task. Psychol Res. 2017 Jan;81(1):271-277. doi: 10.1007/s00426-015-0727-0. Epub 2015 Nov 26. PMID: 26612201; PMCID: PMC5233742.
3. Reedijk SA, Bolders A, Hommel B. The impact of binaural beats on creativity. Front Hum Neurosci. 2013 Nov 14;7:786. doi: 10.3389/fnhum.2013.00786. PMID: 24294202; PMCID: PMC3827550.
4. We only use 10% of our brain:
5. This myth has been debunked by neuroscientists. Here are a few references:
6. https://www.scientificamerican.com/article/do-people-only-use-10-percent-of-their-brains/
7. Division of Sleep Medicine at Harvard Medical School. (2007). Sleep and Disease Risk. Retrieved from https://healthysleep.med.harvard.edu/healthy/matters/consequences/sleep-and-disease-risk
8. Chang, A. M., Aeschbach, D., Duffy, J. F., & Czeisler, C. A. (2015). Evening use of light-emitting eReaders negatively affects sleep, circadian timing, and next-morning alertness. Proceedings of the National Academy of Sciences, 112(4), 1232-1237. doi: 10.1073/pnas.1418490112

9. Chellappa SL, Steiner R, Oelhafen P, Lang D, Götz T, Krebs J, Cajochen C. Acute exposure to evening blue-enriched light impacts on human sleep. J Sleep Res. 2013 Oct;22(5):573-80. doi: 10.1111/jsr.12050. Epub 2013 Mar 20. PMID: 23509952.

10. Shechter A, Kim EW, St-Onge MP, Westwood AJ. Blocking nocturnal blue light for insomnia: A randomized controlled trial. J Psychiatr Res. 2018 Jan;96:196-202. doi: 10.1016/j.jpsychires.2017.10.015. Epub 2017 Oct 21. PMID: 29101797; PMCID: PMC5703049.

11. Okamoto-Mizuno K, Mizuno K. Effects of thermal environment on sleep and circadian rhythm. J Physiol Anthropol. 2012 May 31;31(1):14. doi: 10.1186/1880-6805-31-14. PMID: 22738673; PMCID: PMC3427038.

12. Pham HT, Chuang HL, Kuo CP, Yeh TP, Liao WC. Electronic Device Use before Bedtime and Sleep Quality among University Students. Healthcare (Basel). 2021 Aug 24;9(9):1091. doi: 10.3390/healthcare9091091. PMID: 34574865; PMCID: PMC8466496.

13. Simopoulos AP. An Increase in the Omega-6/Omega-3 Fatty Acid Ratio Increases the Risk for Obesity. Nutrients. 2016 Mar 2;8(3):128. doi: 10.3390/nu8030128. PMID: 26950145; PMCID: PMC4808858.

14. World Health Organization (2018) REPLACE Trans Fat: An Action Package to Eliminate Industrially-Produced Trans-Fatty Acids. https://www.who.int/teams/nutrition-and-food-safety/replace-trans-fat#:~:text=The%20REPLACE%20action%20package%20provides,heart%20disease%20mortality%20and%20events.

15. Smith PJ, Blumenthal JA, Hoffman BM, Cooper H, Strauman TA, Welsh-Bohmer K, Browndyke JN, Sherwood A. Aerobic exercise and neurocognitive performance: a meta-analytic review of randomized controlled trials. Psychosom Med. 2010 Apr;72(3):239-52. doi: 10.1097/PSY.0b013e3181d14633. Epub 2010 Mar 11. PMID: 20223924; PMCID: PMC2897704.

16. Quigley A, MacKay-Lyons M, Eskes G. Effects of Exercise on Cognitive Performance in Older Adults: A Narrative Review of

the Evidence, Possible Biological Mechanisms, and Recommendations for Exercise Prescription. J Aging Res. 2020 May 14;2020:1407896. doi: 10.1155/2020/1407896. PMID: 32509348; PMCID: PMC7244966.

17. Strength-Cognitive Training: A Systemic Review in Adults and Older Adults, and Guidelines to Promote "Strength Exergaming" Innovations
https://www.frontiersin.org/articles/10.3389/fpsyg.2022.855703#.ZEIWBxd7mJY.twitter

18. Liu-Ambrose T, Nagamatsu LS, Graf P, Beattie BL, Ashe MC, Handy TC. Resistance training and executive functions: a 12-month randomized controlled trial. Arch Intern Med. 2010 Jan 25;170(2):170-8. doi: 10.1001/archinternmed.2009.494. PMID: 20101012; PMCID: PMC3448565.

19. Angevaren, Maaike & Aufdemkampe, Geert & Verhaar, H & Aleman, André & Vanhees, Luc. (2008). Physical activity and enhanced fitness to improve cognitive function in older people without known cognitive impairment. Cochrane database of systematic reviews (Online). 2. CD005381. 10.1002/14651858.CD005381.pub3.

20. Leyland LA, Spencer B, Beale N, Jones T, van Reekum CM. The effect of cycling on cognitive function and well-being in older adults. PLoS One. 2019 Feb 20;14(2):e0211779. doi: 10.1371/journal.pone.0211779. PMID: 30785893; PMCID: PMC6388745.

21. Mitten D, Overholt JR, Haynes FI, D'Amore CC, Ady JC. Hiking: A Low-Cost, Accessible Intervention to Promote Health Benefits. Am J Lifestyle Med. 2016 Jul 9;12(4):302-310. doi: 10.1177/1559827616658229. PMID: 32063815; PMCID: PMC6993091.

22. McEwen BS. Physiology and neurobiology of stress and adaptation: central role of the brain. Physiol Rev. 2007 Jul;87(3):873-904. doi: 10.1152/physrev.00041.2006. PMID: 17615391.

23. Rymaszewska J, Lion KM, Pawlik-Sobecka L, Pawłowski T, Szcześniak D, Trypka E, Rymaszewska JE, Zabłocka A,

Stanczykiewicz B. Efficacy of the Whole-Body Cryotherapy as Add-on Therapy to Pharmacological Treatment of Depression-A Randomized Controlled Trial. Front Psychiatry. 2020 Jun 9;11:522. doi: 10.3389/fpsyt.2020.00522. PMID: 32581890; PMCID: PMC7296110.

24. Buijze GA, Sierevelt IN, van der Heijden BC, Dijkgraaf MG, Frings-Dresen MH. The Effect of Cold Showering on Health and Work: A Randomized Controlled Trial. PLoS One. 2016 Sep 15;11(9):e0161749. doi: 10.1371/journal.pone.0161749. Erratum in: PLoS One. 2018 Aug 2;13(8):e0201978. PMID: 27631616; PMCID: PMC5025014.

25. Mori K, Inatomi S, Ouchi K, Azumi Y, Tuchida T. Improving effects of the mushroom Yamabushitake (Hericium erinaceus) on mild cognitive impairment: a double-blind placebo-controlled clinical trial. Phytother Res. 2009 Mar;23(3):367-72. doi: 10.1002/ptr.2634. PMID: 18844328.

26. Nagano, M., Shimizu, K., Kondo, R., Hayashi, C., Sato, D., Kitagawa, K., & Ohnuki, K. (2010). "Reduction of depression and anxiety by 4 weeks Hericium erinaceus intake." Biomedical Research, 31(4), 231-237.

27. Kawamura T, Okubo T, Sato K, Fujita S, Goto K, Hamaoka T, Iemitsu M. Glycerophosphocholine enhances growth hormone secretion and fat oxidation in young adults. Nutrition. 2012 Nov-Dec;28(11-12):1122-6. doi: 10.1016/j.nut.2012.02.011. Epub 2012 Jun 5. PMID: 22673596.

28. Defina PA, Moser RS, Glenn M, Lichtenstein JD, Fellus J. Alzheimer's disease clinical and research update for health care practitioners. J Aging Res. 2013;2013:207178. doi: 10.1155/2013/207178. Epub 2013 Sep 4. PMID: 24083026; PMCID: PMC3776389.

29. Owen GN, Parnell H, De Bruin EA, Rycroft JA. The combined effects of L-theanine and caffeine on cognitive performance and mood. Nutr Neurosci. 2008 Aug;11(4):193-8. doi: 10.1179/147683008X301513. PMID: 18681988.

30. Fitzgerald PJ, Hale PJ, Ghimire A, Watson BO. Repurposing Cholinesterase Inhibitors as Antidepressants? Dose and Stress-

Sensitivity May Be Critical to Opening Possibilities. Front Behav Neurosci. 2021 Jan 14;14:620119. doi: 10.3389/fnbeh.2020.620119. PMID: 33519395; PMCID: PMC7840590.

31. Kumar N, Abichandani LG, Thawani V, Gharpure KJ, Naidu MU, Venkat Ramana G. Efficacy of Standardized Extract of Bacopa monnieri (Bacognize®) on Cognitive Functions of Medical Students: A Six-Week, Randomized Placebo-Controlled Trial. Evid Based Complement Alternat Med. 2016;2016:4103423. doi: 10.1155/2016/4103423. Epub 2016 Oct 10. PMID: 27803728; PMCID: PMC5075615.

32. Hirsch KR, Smith-Ryan AE, Roelofs EJ, Trexler ET, Mock MG. Cordyceps militaris Improves Tolerance to High-Intensity Exercise After Acute and Chronic Supplementation. J Diet Suppl. 2017 Jan 2;14(1):42-53. doi: 10.1080/19390211.2016.1203386. Epub 2016 Jul 13. PMID: 27408987; PMCID: PMC5236007.

33. Tuli HS, Sandhu SS, Sharma AK. Pharmacological and therapeutic potential of Cordyceps with special reference to Cordycepin. 3 Biotech. 2014 Feb;4(1):1-12. doi: 10.1007/s13205-013-0121-9. Epub 2013 Feb 19. PMID: 28324458; PMCID: PMC3909570.

34. Dighriri IM, Alsubaie AM, Hakami FM, Hamithi DM, Alshekh MM, Khobrani FA, Dalak FE, Hakami AA, Alsueaadi EH, Alsaawi LS, Alshammari SF, Alqahtani AS, Alawi IA, Aljuaid AA, Tawhari MQ. Effects of Omega-3 Polyunsaturated Fatty Acids on Brain Functions: A Systematic Review. Cureus. 2022 Oct 9;14(10):e30091. doi: 10.7759/cureus.30091. PMID: 36381743; PMCID: PMC9641984.

35. DiNicolantonio JJ, O'Keefe JH. The Importance of Marine Omega-3s for Brain Development and the Prevention and Treatment of Behavior, Mood, and Other Brain Disorders. Nutrients. 2020 Aug 4;12(8):2333. doi: 10.3390/nu12082333. PMID: 32759851; PMCID: PMC7468918.

36. Cryan, John & Dinan, Timothy. (2012). Cryan, J.F. & Dinan, T.G. Mind-altering microorganisms: the impact of the gut

microbiota on brain and behaviour. Nat. Rev. Neurosci. 13, 701-712. Nature reviews. Neuroscience. 13. 701-12. 10.1038/nrn3346.

37. Mayer EA, Knight R, Mazmanian SK, Cryan JF, Tillisch K. Gut microbes and the brain: paradigm shift in neuroscience. J Neurosci. 2014 Nov 12;34(46):15490-6. doi: 10.1523/JNEUROSCI.3299-14.2014. PMID: 25392516; PMCID: PMC4228144.

38. Kelly JR, Kennedy PJ, Cryan JF, Dinan TG, Clarke G, Hyland NP. Breaking down the barriers: the gut microbiome, intestinal permeability and stress-related psychiatric disorders. Front Cell Neurosci. 2015 Oct 14;9:392. doi: 10.3389/fncel.2015.00392. PMID: 26528128; PMCID: PMC4604320.

39. Zhuang ZQ, Shen LL, Li WW, Fu X, Zeng F, Gui L, Lü Y, Cai M, Zhu C, Tan YL, Zheng P, Li HY, Zhu J, Zhou HD, Bu XL, Wang YJ. Gut Microbiota is Altered in Patients with Alzheimer's Disease. J Alzheimers Dis. 2018;63(4):1337-1346. doi: 10.3233/JAD-180176. PMID: 29758946.

40. Hill, N. (1937). Think and grow rich. Ralston Society.

41. Byrne, R. (2006). The secret. Atria Books.

42. Zhu X, Han Y, Du J, Liu R, Jin K, Yi W. Microbiota-gut-brain axis and the central nervous system. Oncotarget. 2017 May 10;8(32):53829-53838. doi: 10.18632/oncotarget.17754. PMID: 28881854; PMCID: PMC5581153.

43. Šrámek, P., Šimečková, M., Janský, L. et al. Human physiological responses to immersion into water of different temperatures. Eur J Appl Physiol 81, 436–442 (2000). https://doi.org/10.1007/s004210050065

44. Akerstedt T, Knutsson A, Westerholm P, Theorell T, Alfredsson L, Kecklund G. Sleep disturbances, work stress and work hours: a cross-sectional study. J Psychosom Res. 2002 Sep;53(3):741-8. doi: 10.1016/s0022-3999(02)00333-1. PMID: 12217447.

45. Stachenfeld NS, Leone CA, Mitchell ES, Freese E, Harkness L. Water intake reverses dehydration associated impaired executive function in healthy young women. Physiol Behav.

2018 Mar 1;185:103-111. doi: 10.1016/j.physbeh.2017.12.028. Epub 2017 Dec 23. PMID: 29277553.

46. Wikipedia contributors. "Endocrinology." Wikipedia, The Free Encyclopedia. Wikipedia, The Free Encyclopedia, 20 May. 2023. Web. 2 Aug. 2023.

47. Welbourn RB. The emergence of endocrinology. Gesnerus. 1992;49 Pt 2:137-50. PMID: 1398153.

48. Tata JR. One hundred years of hormones. EMBO Rep. 2005 Jun;6(6):490-6. doi: 10.1038/sj.embor.7400444. PMID: 15940278; PMCID: PMC1369102.

49. Otto Loewi – Facts. NobelPrize.org. Nobel Prize Outreach AB 2023. Tue. 8 Aug 2023. <https://www.nobelprize.org/prizes/medicine/1936/loewi/facts/>

50. McCoy AN, Tan SY. Otto Loewi (1873-1961): Dreamer and Nobel laureate. Singapore Med J. 2014 Jan;55(1):3-4. doi: 10.11622/smedj.2014002. PMID: 24452970; PMCID: PMC4291908.

51. Davies KJ. Adaptive homeostasis. Mol Aspects Med. 2016 Jun;49:1-7. doi: 10.1016/j.mam.2016.04.007. Epub 2016 Apr 22. PMID: 27112802; PMCID: PMC4868097.

52. Tabea Tietz, "Walter Bradford Cannon and the Concept of Homeostasis" - http://scihi.org/walter-bradford-cannon-homeostasis/

53. Walter Bradford Cannon. In Wikipedia, retrieved August 8, 2023, from https://en.wikipedia.org/wiki/Walter_Bradford_Cannon

54. Geoffrey Harris (neuroendocrinologist).In Wikipedia, retried August 8, 2023, from https://en.wikipedia.org/wiki/Geoffrey_Harris_(neuroendocrinologist)

55. Walther A, Breidenstein J, Miller R. Association of Testosterone Treatment With Alleviation of Depressive Symptoms in Men: A Systematic Review and Meta-analysis. JAMA Psychiatry. 2019;76(1):31-40. doi:10.1001/jamapsychiatry.2018.2734

56. Andersson AM, Jensen TK, Juul A, Petersen JH, Jørgensen T, Skakkebaek NE. Secular decline in male testosterone and sex

hormone binding globulin serum levels in Danish population surveys. J Clin Endocrinol Metab. 2007;92(12):4696-4705. doi:10.1210/jc.2006-2633

57. Rudolf Clausius. In Wikipedia, retrieved on August 22, 2023, from https://en.wikipedia.org/wiki/Rudolf_Clausius

58. García A, Angel JD, Borrani J, Ramirez C, Valdez P. Sleep deprivation effects on basic cognitive processes: which components of attention, working memory, and executive functions are more susceptible to the lack of sleep? Sleep Sci. 2021 Apr-Jun;14(2):107-118. doi: 10.5935/1984-0063.20200049. PMID: 34381574; PMCID: PMC8340886.

59. McNamara RK, Asch RH, Lindquist DM, Krikorian R. Role of polyunsaturated fatty acids in human brain structure and function across the lifespan: An update on neuroimaging findings. Prostaglandins Leukot Essent Fatty Acids. 2018 Sep;136:23-34. doi: 10.1016/j.plefa.2017.05.001. Epub 2017 May 9. PMID: 28529008; PMCID: PMC5680156.

60. Mehdi S, Manohar K, Shariff A, Kinattingal N, Wani SUD, Alshehri S, Imam MT, Shakeel F, Krishna KL. Omega-3 Fatty Acids Supplementation in the Treatment of Depression: An Observational Study. J Pers Med. 2023 Jan 27;13(2):224. doi: 10.3390/jpm13020224. PMID: 36836458; PMCID: PMC9962071.

61. Krikorian R, Shidler MD, Nash TA, Kalt W, Vinqvist-Tymchuk MR, Shukitt-Hale B, Joseph JA. Blueberry supplementation improves memory in older adults. J Agric Food Chem. 2010 Apr 14;58(7):3996-4000. doi: 10.1021/jf9029332. PMID: 20047325; PMCID: PMC2850944.

62. Katz DL, Doughty K, Ali A. Cocoa and chocolate in human health and disease. Antioxid Redox Signal. 2011 Nov 15;15(10):2779-811. doi: 10.1089/ars.2010.3697. Epub 2011 Jun 13. PMID: 21470061; PMCID: PMC4696435.

63. Spindler M, Beal MF, Henchcliffe C. Coenzyme Q10 effects in neurodegenerative disease. Neuropsychiatr Dis Treat. 2009;5:597-610. doi: 10.2147/ndt.s5212. Epub 2009 Nov 16. PMID: 19966907; PMCID: PMC2785862.

64. Esmaeilzadeh, S., et. al. Front. Psychol., 27 May 2022. Sec. Movement Science. Volume 13 - 2022 | https://doi.org/10.3389/fpsyg.2022.855703
65. Gomes-Osman J, Cabral DF, Morris TP, McInerney K, Cahalin LP, Rundek T, Oliveira A, Pascual-Leone A. Exercise for cognitive brain health in aging: A systematic review for an evaluation of dose. Neurol Clin Pract. 2018 Jun;8(3):257-265. doi: 10.1212/CPJ.0000000000000460. PMID: 30105166; PMCID: PMC6075983.
66. Leyland LA, Spencer B, Beale N, Jones T, van Reekum CM (2019) The effect of cycling on cognitive function and well-being in older adults. PLOS ONE 14(2): e0211779. https://doi.org/10.1371/journal.pone.0211779
67. Clapp M, Aurora N, Herrera L, Bhatia M, Wilen E, Wakefield S. Gut microbiota's effect on mental health: The gut-brain axis. Clin Pract. 2017 Sep 15;7(4):987. doi: 10.4081/cp.2017.987. PMID: 29071061; PMCID: PMC5641835.
68. Taniya MA, Chung HJ, Al Mamun A, Alam S, Aziz MA, Emon NU, Islam MM, Hong SS, Podder BR, Ara Mimi A, Aktar Suchi S, Xiao J. Role of Gut Microbiome in Autism Spectrum Disorder and Its Therapeutic Regulation. Front Cell Infect Microbiol. 2022 Jul 22;12:915701. doi: 10.3389/fcimb.2022.915701. PMID: 35937689; PMCID: PMC9355470.

Made in the USA
Columbia, SC
27 September 2023